SOMEONE ONCE SAID

Words of Wisdom and Advice for Law Enforcement Supervisors, Managers, and Leaders

JOHN ANDERSON

Fresno, California

Someone Once Said

Copyright © 2022 by John Anderson

All rights reserved. No part of this publication may be reproduced, stored in a retrieval system, or transmitted in any form by means, electronic, mechanical, photocopying, recording or otherwise, without the prior written permission of the author.

Published by Quill Driver Books,
an imprint of Linden Publishing
2006 South Mary Street, Fresno, California 93721
(559) 233-6633 / (800) 345-4447
QuillDriverBooks.com

Quill Driver Books and colophon are trademarks of
Linden Publishing, Inc.

Linden Publishing titles may be purchased in quantity at special discounts for educational, business, or promotional use. To inquire about discount pricing, please refer to the contact information above. For permission to use any portion of this book for academic purposes, please contact the Copyright Clearance Center at www.copyright.com.

ISBN 978-0-578-94983-3

135798642

Printed in the United States of America
on acid-free paper.

Book design by Carla Green, Clarity Designworks.

Library of Congress Cataloging-in-Publication Data on file.

CONTENTS

PREFACE

When examining organizations, the most studied, lectured-on, and written-about subjects we encounter are the art and skills of supervising, managing, and leading people, all of which mesh together so that the goals and objectives of the organization can be accomplished. Even if you haven't started up the chain, what is contained here may assist you career-wise and give you some idea of what the upper echelons are about.

Law enforcement is one of the most difficult but necessary professions today. It is the primary entity that safeguards our citizens and protects communities from utter chaos, permitting us a somewhat civilized living. Therefore, it is vitally important that law enforcement agencies be supervised, managed, and led in the most efficient and professional manner possible. This book is dedicated to those who try to do just that.

SOMEONE ONCE SAID:

Blessed are the peacekeepers, for they shall be called the children of God.
—Matthew 5:9

INTRODUCTION

If you are like most of us, when you entered the work world, you started at the bottom of the organization. As time passed, if you were a good employee, openings further up the chain occurred, and if you had the desire, you may have been given the opportunity to advance to a more complex or important assignment.

Promotion is quite likely something that you have strived to achieve. It normally includes a raise in pay, increased responsibility, and an elevated status in the organization. It also usually entails supervision of others and may offer the ability to make changes you deem necessary. In law enforcement, you are normally promoted from officer or deputy to corporal or sergeant. Then later on up the ladder, you advance to lieutenant, captain, chief, colonel, or superintendent.

SOMEONE ONCE SAID:

**By working faithfully eight hours a day,
you may eventually become a boss,
and can now work twelve hours a day.**
—Robert Frost

In most cases, upon your initial promotion you will be offered the opportunity to, or required to, attend a class in basic supervision. If this is the case, you are lucky. That training will provide you with the basics.

Unfortunately, though, in-house courses conducted by a law enforcement organization are often centered on the rules and regulations of the host department or agency, and the core essentials of supervision, management, and leadership are minimized.

Maybe while growing up you were lucky enough to have gained some supervisory experience as a class officer or sports team captain. The decisions that you were called on to make normally had little consequence. There were always adults, teachers, or coaches to assist you in basic supervision and decision making.

Or maybe while in the military you were a leader of some sort. The advantage of that position was that your subordinates were probably conditioned to accept authority and did not place blame on you for dismal working conditions and the consistently autocratic leadership style.

In any case, if you do attend a formal or agency-sponsored class or even a college course, you will be given instruction based on the teachings and experiences of those who have enjoyed supervisory success and are considered experts.

Most often this training will be given not only at the initial supervisory level but at each successive rank that you achieve. If it is not given as part of the promotional process, you should try to acquire it on your own.

Through this reading you will be exposed to the ideas and thoughts of the legendary management gurus whose beliefs, theories, and findings have been taught and written about endlessly and pretty much proven through actual use. Some are considered classics.

All of these concepts are important, and they all deal with basically the same topics in similar but occasionally dissimilar ways. Their purpose is to provide instruction in how to become better supervisors, managers, and leaders.

But do understand that even though we have the benefit of guidance and instruction from these supervisory, management, and leadership experts, we must be aware that application of the various theories and methods must be done in the real world, in today's ever-changing world.

Throughout this book, the learnings and teachings of these many experts will be discussed, quoted, and referenced to the law enforcement environment.

Also included are fairly accurate tales of application and misapplication of these theories by police supervisors, managers, and leaders. They are not "cops-and-robbers" stories but applicable occurrences, some having successful and some not so successful outcomes.

The law enforcement field is rapidly changing, and although some concepts and theories of the experts appear to be dated and may even be so, hopefully exposure to them will assist you in your career and performance as you learn from what

SOMEONE ONCE SAID

SUPERVISION, MANAGEMENT, AND LEADERSHIP FOR LAW ENFORCEMENT

Compared with other professions, being a supervisor, manager, or leader in law enforcement is different and appreciably more difficult. This is because the field of law enforcement is oftentimes dangerous and complex, change is a constant, and very little becomes routine.

SOMEONE ONCE SAID:

In law enforcement, quite often the measure of success is the intangible and the immeasurable, or just what doesn't happen.
—Author

This means that for a police agency, the profit motive is absent and the number of widgets produced is not tallied, so success is not so easily measured. Comparative statistics can offer some sort of gauge of success or not, but comparing year-by-year results is often inaccurate because conditions do not stay the same.

Financial factors change as do populations and their makeup. The simple incorporation of a district or neighborhood can drastically change the size and makeup of the citizenry in both the acquiring and losing jurisdictions, thereby making comparisons invalid. Crime is people related. As the number, types, and character of the population changes, so do the number, types, and characteristics of crimes.

Legislative change which adds or removes criminal statutes makes past and present comparisons almost impossible. For instance, the legalization of marijuana in some jurisdictions has greatly affected crime and arrest stats in those districts. The courts can also impact crime statistics. A single judicial decision can make legal what was formerly prohibited or vice versa.

Add to this the fact that unlike private businesses or corporations, police agencies, because of their placement in government, are not led by or owned by people who are familiar with the product. In the private sector, the owners or administrators have either built or risen through the organization. Others may have been laterally hired from a similar type of business or company. In any case, these administrators have learned what the business is about and possess an intricate knowledge of its operation.

Conversely, law enforcement agencies may on the surface appear to be led by a chief, sheriff, or someone of similar rank, but in fact they are actually controlled by, and must answer to, others in government who, for the most part, know little or nothing about law enforcement—mayors, city councils or managers, boards of supervisors, police commissions, and ultimately the public.

Those in charge at the state and federal levels include governors, legislators, attorney generals, and even presidents. They are even further removed from the streets and the profession.

In most cases, these individuals have limited or no knowledge of the operation of a law enforcement agency, but their lack of understanding doesn't preclude or restrict them from assuming management roles. They influence and most times control the budgeting, planning, human resources, and overall operation and ultimate control of the agency.

As you can imagine, this makes it harder for the chief, sheriff, or whoever to oversee the actual operation of the organization, which by its nature is already a difficult task.

SOMEONE ONCE SAID:

Organizations generally have three levels of governance; supervisors, middle managers, and leaders.
—Anonymous

A governmental agency can have many more.

Dozens of management books have been written, hundreds of classes taught, and speeches given on these three identified levels of supervision, management, and leadership and on how to be successful in each.

As this book examines the various management levels and their responsibilities, it will present the principles and recommended practices of those who have written those books, taught those classes, and given those speeches.

The accepted mechanics that make up the factors for success at each level, such as motivation, planning, organizing, directing, and so on, will be discussed, as will potential problems that may be encountered.

Most of the areas examined will be a general overview; however, some, because of their importance and relevance, will be presented in greater detail.

Hopefully, by considering some of the thoughts and experiences of these recognized experts and adopting their recommendations, as you advance through the ranks, you can lessen or avoid some of the difficulties, concerns, and potential mistakes in your police management career and become a more successful law enforcement supervisor, manager, and leader.

SUPERVISION

So you want to be or maybe are going to be a supervisor. After applying yourself diligently to study and sweating through both the written and oral examinations, or whatever type of testing torment your department uses to select supervisors, you made it and the day for sewing on the stripes has arrived.

SOMEONE ONCE SAID:

The sergeant is the Army.
—*General Dwight D. Eisenhower*

As a new supervisor, you may have some uncertainties and doubts about your competence, knowledge, and ability to function at the new level. Your technical knowledge must be adequate—you passed the tests, didn't you? But how about your ability to supervise people? In your studies you became acquainted with the labels of accepted management theories and should know something about chains of command, spans of control, unity of command, and authority commensurate with whatever. And although these are time-tested principles that will serve you well, you may still have some personal misgivings.

What follows may be a different set of supervisory ideas that may possibly be of some assistance to you, though they are not as close to canonization as those given you in a basic supervision class. Perhaps their real value is that they do not depend on universal application throughout the organization in order to be successful. In other words, you can apply the identified principles and concepts yourself. They may not be used by others in your agency, but they can be known to and used by you exclusively and independently. And applied in that fashion they will improve your management abilities and be of value to the organization as a whole.

Supervision is primarily the practice of observing those who serve under you and attempting to assure that they are doing what management expects them to do. The International Association of Chiefs of Police (IACP) some time ago advised that one of law enforcement's basic duties is to encourage "voluntary compliance" with the nation's laws. This same approach can be used in assuring that employees obey the organization's rules and orders and give a day's work for a day's pay.

This concept of voluntary compliance can be achieved by those in charge of applying the basic principles of human guidance that are discussed in this writing. It's kind of like parenting.

THE BASICS

SOMEONE ONCE SAID:

The job changes, not the person.
—Author

If you work in a small department, you have the advantage of knowing the people you will be working for, with, and supervising. This is both good and bad. You probably know the idiosyncrasies and potentials of those both above and below you in rank and have some idea of what to expect. But they also know you.

With respect to those whom you will be supervising, you should have a pretty good idea of their work habits and skill and knowledge levels. You should be familiar enough with them, and they with you, to have already established a working relationship.

However, one problem may be that they also recall some of your work habits and past incidents of which you may not be proud. Be that as it may, you now have a job to do. The past is the past and you can't change it, but you can endeavor not to repeat past mistakes. Just as your subordinates may not forget your misdeeds, you need not forget theirs. Don't use this information to pursue a vendetta, but keep it in mind as a tool to assist you in eliciting correct behavior in the future. For instance, if you are aware that one of your troops frequently leaves the beat to conduct personal business, this awareness may assist you in limiting missed calls and slow responses on that officer's part. Use both positive and negative information that you possess to make your job easier and the organization better.

SOMEONE ONCE SAID:

The only thing more dangerous than ignorance is arrogance.

—Albert Einstein

One common mistake new supervisors make is the feeling of self-magnificence and amour propre that comes with a personal triumph such as a promotion.

As can be imagined, quite often this has a negative effect on the relationship between the new supervisor and his or her subordinates.

Remember, even though you now, because of your new position, have a greater amount of authority and take home a larger paycheck, you are still the same person that you were. You have the same strengths and weaknesses, suffer from the same delusions, and possess the identical virtues. No magic spell was cast or wand waved to greatly expand your knowledge or increase your intelligence and abilities. Those stripes don't always make you right.

Unfortunately, some promotes are not initially aware of this, and some, as they rise through the ranks, never become aware of it. For these folks, appropriate advice might be to buy a larger hat along with the new chevrons, but don't plan on being happy wearing either.

SOMEONE ONCE SAID:

Rank does not confer privilege or give power. It imposes responsibility.

—Peter Drucker

Be yourself—the same person you always were! Emulate the admirable traits and qualities of your superiors and more experienced peers, but do it as you. Some of them may utilize a style that doesn't fit your personality or type. In other words, copy their good qualities and abilities, but don't adopt their persona.

Don't be afraid to admit your shortcomings and own up to your mistakes. As an officer, you most likely went to senior officers for answers. In most matters, it is no disgrace to continue this practice and go to more experienced peers.

Remember, however, that not all of those working with you have totally admirable qualities. Their supervisory methods may work for them but not for you.

ONCE UPON A TIME,
in a fairly large-size department a newly promoted sergeant was placed in a smaller specialized unit in a non-patrol division. The division was commanded by a lieutenant who had a pretty loud type A personality. He knew that he was the boss, and he expected everyone else to know it too. His management style was arrogant and brash.

Upon their initial meeting the lieutenant took the new sergeant into his office and pretty much shouted out his expectations, leaving the sergeant shell-shocked and wondering how long he would have to wait before putting in a transfer to another unit.

Although short in duration, this initial encounter had extremely negative results. It created an expectation in the sergeant's mind that he should act just like the lieutenant, and when he did so, it had the expected negative effect on his subordinates.

In a short time the assigned officers became rebellious. They weren't outright disobedient or unmanageable, but they causally resisted almost every direction and set a record for the filing of grievances. Every act even slightly in error committed by the new sergeant was complained about to higher-ups in writing. Production in the unit also suffered.

The supervisor whom the newly promoted sergeant had replaced had retired early for stress-related medical reasons, but in his last couple of years he had pretty much kept a low profile, knowing he was on his way out.

Because the lieutenant had somewhat kept his distance from day-to-day operations, his style had little influence on the officers, and because they were assigned to a specialized unit, they were motivated to perform at a high level.

Now, however, faced with the new sergeant's somewhat tyrannical approach, things went awry. The sergeant's approach was not the only thing affecting the officers. One of them had partnered with him years back and on graveyard they had occasionally "cribbed" (slept in the patrol car). He made this known to the group, concluding that the stripes had gone to his former partner's head and he had become a real jerk.

Headquarters soon became aware of the discontent and took notice of the large number of complaints, petty grievances, and reduction in the unit's output. They called the lieutenant on the carpet, and he of course placed blame on the new sergeant.

As a result, the sergeant's probationary period was extended and he was reassigned to the field. He was also directed to attend a class on human relations. That class saved his job. He learned of his errors and resolved to supervise in his own style. Management eventually learned of the lieutenant's failings and he was reassigned.

This example illustrates that positive supervisory practices are important and that you must perform in your own style utilizing your own personality.

SOMEONE ONCE SAID:

Pick your role models wisely.
—Lana Del Rey

You might have to live with some of your past actions, but remember the past is past, that was then, this is now, and it is now that counts.

In summation, don't try to be a different person. Apparently, your current knowledge skills and abilities were sufficient to be considered for advancement. You haven't changed. Only your job has changed.

SOMEONE ONCE SAID:

To be yourself in a world that is constantly trying to make you something else is the greatest accomplishment.
—*Ralph Waldo Emerson*

You may also be working side by side with those who previously supervised you. They, too, will have knowledge of your past, both your strong and weak points. In dealing with them, remember that because of their seniority in grade and experience as a supervisor, at least initially they are sure to know more about the position than you do. Give them some respect.

SOMEONE ONCE SAID:

Respecting someone indicates the quality of your character.
—*Mohammad Rishad Sakhi*

If you haven't already, befriend them. You can certainly learn from their experience. And remember, they may be ahead of you in getting the next promotion and you may find yourself working for them again.

POSITIVE DIRECTION

People working in the criminal justice field are, for the most part, hired after an extensive screening process in which their ability to exercise independent thought and judgment was a major consideration. Their facility to exhibit forthright individualism was considered a virtue. Daily, the citizenry must rely on the capabilities of these officers to act correctly and competently, often in emergencies or under high stress, and for the most part, the officers do so, both efficiently and dependably.

If the foregoing is true, why do many police supervisors expect their subordinates to act like sheep and treat them accordingly?

Supervisors and managers who stifle initiative by promulgating meaningless arbitrary directives, who insist on making every decision, and who are unwilling to delegate or entrust subordinates with authority might be better off with a shepherd's staff than a sergeant's stripes.

Somewhere along the line they have gotten off track in their roles and responsibilities. For the most part, the job of a supervisor is to be supportive and to assist and guide the people actually doing the work. Anything a supervisor can do to make the task easier or to assist in its accomplishment should be the goal.

This, by the way, is true for all levels of management.

Simply stated, in most cases, employees should be told what needs to be done, and if they are competent, how it gets done should be left up to them.

Another point: be careful in giving orders. Directives prefaced by a "Would you mind?" or "Will you please?" carry the same weight as an expressed command but are more readily accepted and obeyed.

SOMEONE ONCE SAID:

A good leader avoids issuing orders, preferring to request, imply, or make suggestions.
—Abraham Lincoln

This kinder, gentler approach and its value will be further discussed.

When presented with a question or problem from a subordinate, all too often a supervisor will display an attitude of impatience that implies "Don't bother me" or "This is something you should know!"

A more effective response is "What do you think?" or "Have you got any ideas?"

Not only does this involve subordinates in the decision-making process and perhaps stimulates their gray matter, it often provides insight into their rationale and knowledge level. Plus, it can do much to enhance your mutual relationship. They may even go away thinking, "The sergeant cares about what I think."

Also, you may be amazed at some of the remarkable solutions they are able to come up with. Things that you never thought of.

SOMEONE ONCE SAID:

Criticize with care, help each other be right, not wrong.
—Anonymous

One of your primary responsibilities as an officer was to observe the public and make judgments on whether their behavior was lawful or not. For the most part, your job was to discover wrong-doing and most of your training and efforts followed this vein. For example, a traffic officer does not ordinarily stop motorists who are obeying the law. Energy and effort are directed at drivers who are *not* obeying the law.

In the police field it is very easy to carry this "error orientation" over to the supervisory role, which results in a negative approach to management.

SOMEONE ONCE SAID:

Don't find fault, find a remedy.
—Henry Ford

Care must be taken to, as they say, "accentuate the positive" while not totally "ignoring the negative." Don't make absolute perfection the central issue in your supervisory role. When criticism is due, one might be wise to use the method employed by most successful traffic cops— condemn the act committed rather than the person committing it.

For example, officers are encouraged to say something like:

"Sir, I stopped you for speeding, that is a very dangerous violation, and you could become involved in an accident."

Rather than:

"Sir, I stopped you for speeding, and you should not be committing such a dangerous violation because you are endangering yourself and others."

There's not much difference in the wording, but the meaning and emphasis have been altered through the slight change in dialogue. The point is that we want the violator thinking "Speed is bad" rather than "That officer called me bad."

This same approach can be used when correcting subordinates. Place the blame on the act, not the person committing it. This works very well when dealing with traffic violators and can lower the emotional and stress levels when addressing issues with subordinates as well.

Another way of making a negative pill easier to swallow is to open the "corrective" discussions with pleasantries and commendatory remarks. Then close the discussions in the same manner, with the critical and corrective statements sandwiched in between.

This gentler versus autocratic supervisory method was recommended by the management theorist and social psychologist **Douglas McGregor** in his book *The Human Side of Enterprise*. In it, he identified what he termed the "Theory X and Theory Y" approaches to supervision.

McGregor described Theory X as an authoritarian style of management. Utilizing this seemingly negative methodology, a supervisor assumes that it's natural for people not to really like work and will try to avoid it. Further, that because of this, they must be closely monitored and be threatened with punishment in order for them to perform. Under Theory X, it is believed that workers' continued salary and job security are most important to them and that by threatening these, compliance and greater effort will result.

Many supervisors recognize this as an easy approach to controlling subordinates and utilize it. They create an overly strict environment by establishing petty rules and strictly enforcing them. Over time, the workers get used to the environment and submit to being treated like sheep. The employees will work, but only through fear of the negative consequences if they do not. And they will mostly do only the minimum required to get by.

To Theory X supervisors, following the rules is of primary importance, even more so than accomplishing goals. And if things go wrong, the Theory X supervisor looks only to place blame. Quite often discipline and punishment follow.

Under Theory X supervision, production may be steady but improvement is rare. In some cases, employees, rather than trying to improve, seek ways to work less and coast when they can.

SOMEONE ONCE SAID:

The ingenuity of the average worker is sufficient to outwit any system of controls devised by management.
—Douglas McGregor

More plainly, if employees want to, they can circumvent oppressive rules and management's adverse attitudes.

Conversely, McGregor's Theory Y suggests a more cooperative approach by management. In this method, termed "participative management," he compared work with play. McGregor believed that by making the workplace friendlier and less hostile, employees, on their own initiative, would work harder and seek responsibility because they enjoyed being there. Human nature and accomplishment alone are what motivate people to want to succeed. And if rewarded, they will work even harder.

Thus, by creating a climate and environment where people want to succeed, can succeed, and are rewarded when they do, management will help the entire organization benefit and be successful also.

So how do we create that participative climate where the workers want to and can assume more responsibility and are motivated to do more and strive to succeed?

SOMEONE ONCE SAID:

Treat your people like you want them to treat the public.
—Author

One method of creating this participative climate is by sharing your knowledge with workers and hopefully expanding their interest and understanding of the job. This isn't accomplished by telling "war stories," but by challenging them and giving them additional responsibility. If questions arise regarding the law, court decisions, or just what to do in certain situations, encourage them to do the research and come up with the answers. Then praise them when they do. This is how schoolteachers operate and maintain the interest of their students.

This can be accomplished formally or informally. The greater interest they take in their job and the more informed they become in the "whats and whys" concerning their work environment, the easier your job will become.

ONCE UPON A TIME,
a commander was asked to sit on a Qualifications Appraisal Panel (oral board) for a middle-size sister agency. This department was conducting interviews for an open lieutenant's position and had narrowed the field down to three candidates. All were given the following question: What have you done to prepare yourself for promotion?

The first candidate responded that he had purposely scheduled himself for the night shift so that he could attend college in hopes of obtaining a degree in police science.

Candidate number two's answer was that she had taken every opportunity to attend all available police-related seminars and technical courses on her own time for the most part. This had really increased her professional knowledge and made her a better supervisor.

The third candidate said, "I just tried to be the very best sergeant I could be. I did this by developing and instructing our officers. At every briefing, I would select a statute or departmental order to quiz the officers on. After a while, it became kind of a game, and they would try to stump me. I learned and they learned. That experience expanded my knowledge and that of my subordinates."

The oral board selected the third candidate for promotion.

In summation, in your daily encounters with your subordinates, be aware of the importance of positive interpersonal relations and try to utilize McGregor's suggested participative approach.

These small strategies will pay off.

KNOW YOUR PEOPLE

SOMEONE ONCE SAID:

People who need people are the luckiest people in the world.
—Barbra Streisand

Admittedly, it is difficult to really know the people who work for you well, but it is worthwhile to make the effort to learn as much as you can about them. This can be done by studying their personnel files as they will contain information about your workers' backgrounds and their families. If nothing else, this will give you a starting point when talking to them. Also, you might find that you have some common interests that will provide a discussion area.

Knowing even the bare minimum about your subordinates may give you some insight into what causes their behavior, both good and bad. Also, maybe their likes and dislikes. You may learn what pleases them and motivates them. Having this knowledge will make your supervision of them easier and more effective.

Let's say you discover that an employee is a veteran. This should tell you that he or she is somewhat conditioned to taking orders and understands the concepts of unit cohesiveness and the chain of command. Thus, you will not have to spend a great deal of time explaining every reason for every directive from above. This employee is used to being told what to do and to follow orders without a lot of questions.

Maybe you will observe that one of your subordinates has gone through more than a couple of marriages or has had some citizen complaints. This could indicate that the individual may have interpersonal relations problems. Being aware of this can be helpful.

You may learn that your subordinates graduated from college or even grad school. If so, maybe they can teach you a thing or two.

None of these observations are absolute, but they just may provide you with some insight into individuals and make your job of understanding and supervising them easier.

The next step should be arranging to have some "one-on-one" time with them. For example, you can conduct ride-a-longs or meet with them for lunch or coffee.

Initially, you may find that some of them might be standoffish and not very relaxed. This is to be expected. After all, you are their supervisor, and if they don't know you well, it is natural for them to suspect that the meeting is to discuss a problem or something they may have done wrong.

You can attempt to dispel this feeling by being friendly and complimenting them on something that they have recently done—a good arrest, a well-done report or investigation, or just looking sharp in their uniform. Any of these will, as they say, "break the ice."

After a few such informal meetings, you should be able to discover their interests and what motivates them. You might even discuss their future plans and goals.

Your knowing just the basics in these areas will improve your ability to properly supervise them and make your job easier. Plus, by displaying an interest in them, you are utilizing McGregor's Theory Y.

SOMEONE ONCE SAID:

One must talk little and listen much.
—African proverb

Remember, the conversation should be about them, not about you.

SOMEONE ONCE SAID:

Everybody likes something.
—Anonymous

If you know and believe this and are able to discover your subordinates' interests, you can reduce your problems as a supervisor. All human beings (even officers) no matter how calloused, how outwardly cynical or withdrawn, are interested in something. It may be themselves, it may be baseball, or it may be the friendly server in the coffee shop. But each of us has something in which we have a genuine interest.

Fortunately, in most cases, particularly early in our career, it is the job. It is interesting, exciting, rewarding, and something we enjoy doing.

There is, however, a tendency after a few years of experience to lose a little of that interest, and officers believing themselves to be veterans tend to slow down in their playing of the game. Cops and robbers may not hold the same fascination that it once did.

This then is where one of the basic management principles called "motivation" kicks in. At one point in our career we were highly motivated and even would have worked for nothing if we could have afforded it. But with the passing of time, this desire may have waned.

There are numerous thoughts and beliefs about how people can be motivated. Some are simple, others more complex. But the basic principle is that the more highly motivated your subordinates are, whatever the reason, the easier your job will be.

The fundamental responsibility of a supervisor is to get the job done. The difficulty is that you must now get it done through other people. When you were the worker, you probably had a high interest in the job and wanted to do it as well as you could. If the people you supervise are similarly motivated, your job will be much easier. Unfortunately, this is not always the case. Some may have lost that high interest.

Knowing your people, their interests, and their likes and dislikes can get you started in bringing them around.

ONCE UPON A TIME,
there was an officer who through time had lost his zeal for the job. This was evident through his frequent use of sick leave, his habit of being the last to report for shift and hit the beat, and being the first out of the door after work. His reports and investigations in general, although adequate, were lackluster. His demeanor was seemingly indifferent. As can be imagined, an attitude such as this was cause for concern, not just for productivity but for officer safety.

A supervisor noting this decided to determine the cause. This was easy. The employee had lost job interest.

So the supervisor began some one-on-one observations of the officer, taking every opportunity to engage in conversation, conduct ride-a-longs, and share lunch and coffee breaks. Even with the supervisor present, the officer's job interest and energy were lacking.

However, the supervisor did learn one thing. The officer was crazy about kids. Although his marriage was childless, he was very involved in Little League Baseball and scouting. Wisely recognizing this "interest" of the officer, the supervisor attempted to channel it toward the job. He requested him to assist in developing and presenting a bicycle safety program for elementary-level students.

Although the officer had no staff experience and had not previously made any public presentations, he let himself be talked into giving it a try.

The results were truly amazing! The program developed was excellent! It was expanded to neighboring communities and was eventually featured on a local television channel. The officer was invited to make a presentation before a local school board, which incorporated the program and the officer into its elementary school curriculum.

The change in the officer's performance improved substantially. His attitude and enthusiasm toward his job were renewed, and he once again became a productive employee.

This story in itself serves to reinforce the point that "everybody likes something," and if a supervisor can discover what it is and somehow apply it to the job, a positive change in behavior is possible. Again, this comes from knowing your people!

Once an employee shows an increased interest in some facet of the job, even though it is not necessarily included in the basic job description, and is given the responsibility to perform and accomplish the task, it normally follows that overall job performance will improve. Thus we have McGregor's positive method and Theory Y at work.

This approach is consistent with another theory called "job enrichment," which will be discussed later.

GETTING ALONG

Another point to be made with regard to being an effective supervisor is that you should realize that not everyone will like you and some of the things that you do. This is human nature. It is also true that you will not necessarily like all of the people that you supervise. Knowing this doesn't diminish the fact that you must treat all of your subordinates equally.

This can be difficult as they will range throughout the spectrum in capability, intelligence, job interest, personality, and just plain likability. There will be differences in sex, race, religion, and educational and family background. With some subordinates, even though diversity exists, there will be no problem, but with others, you may have daily conflict. A lot of the time minor hostility may arise from something in their past. For example, they may feel that management unfairly treated them and you are partly to blame. This is something that you cannot go back and change, yet if it is affecting their work, it must be addressed.

But before you start trying to change them, look at yourself. Perhaps you are inadvertently antagonizing them by some mannerisms or actions they believe to be offensive. But if you are not receiving the similar negativity from others you supervise, the problem is probably that individual's.

The Golden Rule about treating others as you would like to be treated might be a place to start in trying to get along. The proposed informal coffee meetings and ride-a-longs might bring out common interests and areas for civil discourse with those people whom you have some sort of personality problem with. If that doesn't work, perhaps a discussion with them about whatever differences you seem to have. Sometimes people don't realize how they are affecting others.

By talking to them, perhaps you can determine whether it's just you or authority in general that they are resisting. Or it may be that they just have a contrary personality.

Whatever the case, you must do your best not to treat them any differently than you treat your stars.

SOMEONE ONCE SAID:

Everybody counts or nobody counts.
—Detective Harry Bosch

Remember, though, your job is to improve job performance. Unless these individuals' attitude is negatively affecting their or others' work, or how they interact with the public, it is sometimes better just to live with it and concentrate on solvable problems.

MOTIVATION

If it is true that success brings happiness, you would think that the desire for happiness would be incentive enough for employees to work hard, do well, and fulfill their obligations. But unfortunately, as has been stated, that's not always the case.

As we have evolved from hunters-gatherers to agrarian, industrial, and now electronic/high-tech societies, the need to produce to survive has pretty much disappeared. Consequently, it is believed, perhaps correctly so, that humankind's need to exert maximum energy and effort for survival need not be present.

From the early 1900s until today, experts have studied the means and methods to get increased production in the workplace. Subsequently, various so-called motivational theories have evolved.

One of the first recognized management theorists was **Abraham Maslow**. Born in 1908, he became a noted psychologist who through the study of monkeys established the belief that all living organisms have basic needs and that these organisms are motivated to fill these needs merely for survival. Once a need is met, other needs emerge, depending on the level of the organism's development.

Examining human behavior, Maslow identified five levels of needs, which he arranged in a hierarchy that he described in his article "A Theory of Human Motivation."

He began with what he termed "physiological needs": air to breath, water to drink, and food to eat. The basic essentials for life.

Next he listed "safety and security," addressing the requirement for suitable lodging and methods of protection.

Following these are what he termed "social needs": the requirement to belong in a community or group and an individual's need to be recognized in that group.

Last, Maslow identified what he termed the state of "self-actualization." This is the stage where a person has fulfilled the basic security and social needs, is enjoying the success of living, and has achieved, as he describes it, "what a man can be, he must be." More plainly, an individual has attained their major goal or place in life.

Maslow's theory is important because it instructs us to try to identify what a person's needs are and, once identified, gives guidance on what has to be done to fulfill or at least accommodate them. By knowing this, we can assist the individual in meeting those needs and motivate the individual to progress on up the hierarchy. This motivation results in their improved interest, their trying harder and accomplishing more. All of which improves them as an employee and increase their value to the organization.

It is probably correct to say that you and most of those you supervise are elevated above the basic levels of survival, having adequate sustenance and a reasonably secure place to live.

Maslow's identified second level was achieved by your having a position with an adequate salary and benefits. However, there will be officers still trying to fill this need by taking on a second job or working all available overtime.

Affable working conditions, absent favoritism, harassment, excessive strictness, and pettiness, can fill this social need. Quite often employee groups, team sports, or even union activities contribute to meeting this need.

Proper management, employee recognition, and advancement opportunities help meet the self-esteem requirements.

SOMEONE ONCE SAID:

People's behavior makes sense if you think about it in terms of their goals, needs, and motives.

—Thomas Mann

More recently, another noted psychologist, **Clayton Alderfer**, expanded on Maslow's beliefs in a book titled *Existence, Relatedness, and Growth: Human Needs in Organizational Settings*. Alderfer's existence, relatedness, and growth (ERG) theory reduces the needs hierarchy to three levels. Existence is primarily the basic needs of food shelter and safety. He explained that relatedness includes the need for love and social belonging. The growth level includes possessing a personality trait that has the need for self-esteem.

ERG differs from Maslow's thoughts in that Alderfer claimed that the fulfillment of the needs do not have to be addressed in a hierarchal order. Thus management seeking to motivate an individual need not start at the bottom of the list. If you discover that an individual favorably responds to praise and recognition, even though he or she may not be a "groupie" as a requisite in the relatedness category, this is OK. Motivate them through praise and recognition, and don't concern yourself with their not belonging or engaging in group activities. Or again, they might be at the existence level and can be motivated by physical rewards such as a salary increase or paid time off.

Some experts believe that the flexibility offered by Alderfer is superior to Maslow's strict hierarchy.

In either case, the bottom line is determining what a person's needs are and attempting to satisfy those needs in the work environment.

Another pair of psychologists, **Edward Deci** and *Richard Ryan*, have examined what has been termed the essence of motivation.

They divided motivation into two distinct categories: "intrinsic" and "extrinsic."

In their book *Intrinsic Motivation*, Edward Deci describes intrinsic motivation as an energizing behavior that comes from within an individual, out of will and interest for the activity at hand. No outside rewards are required to incite the person into action. Participation in sports, just for the fun of doing so, is an example of intrinsic motivation.

These intrinsic factors make us want to accomplish something for personal reasons. They include a strong desire to complete a task, a need for acceptance, a pursuit of power, and recognition and acquisition of a higher social status and appreciation.

In contrast, the extrinsic motivators are basically monetary in nature; more pay means a better standard of living, a nicer house, a faster car, and free time spent in a desired but more expensive fashion. Extrinsic factors also include performing tasks to avoid a penalty, such as losing one's job or position.

Various studies have indicated that both types are true motivators, but both have some failings. Oftentimes the motivation of the intrinsic becomes stale and the enthusiasm wanes due to repetitive actions. Apparently, employees tire of doing the same thing over and over and receiving the same nonmonetary rewards. A person only has so many walls on which to hang certificates. Again, the "old timer" example discussed previously would fall in this group as one who has lost his intrinsic motivation.

As was done in that case, perhaps management should examine the job and see if any changes can be made to revitalize the employee's interest. Varying the types and forms of recognition and rewards should also be looked at.

The "extrinsic" needs/rewards approach also may have a drawback. Studies have shown that college students who were given valued prizes for success in class apparently tired of the effort once the prize was received. With nothing to look forward to, the students' performance diminished. The belief in this case is that the rewards have to be continual in order for the increased effort to continue. Public agencies may have difficulty in continuing or increasing monetary rewards.

Something to be considered, though, might be specialty pay programs, such as assignment to motorcycles, task forces, and so on.

As we continue, several other theories and ideas for motivating our employees will be discussed. Remember, if something doesn't work, try something else and continue to try. Everybody needs or likes something. It is your job to discover what those needs or interests are and to try to fulfill those needs or associate those interests with the position's responsibilities.

SOMEONE ONCE SAID:

It is management's job to create a climate where people want to succeed, where they can succeed, and to reward them when they do succeed.
—Author

So how do you do that? How do you create that climate?

As a first-line supervisor you exist in an organizational climate that for the most part has been created by those above you.

Someone "up there" has established the rules and policies that govern the operation of the agency. They might be general, or they might be precise and inflexible.

In either case, what is universal is that members of the department are expected to abide by and obey them, usually without question. This was pretty much the agreement you made when you accepted the job. And now, as a member of the management team, whether you agree with them or not, it is now your job not only to comply with the rules but to enforce them.

SOMEONE ONCE SAID:

Hold people accountable, but give them the tools to succeed.
—Howard Schultz

So, to start to create that climate, remember when disciplining, try to condemn the act rather than the person committing it. Always reward good behavior. Just a "Thanks, good job" or "Well done" goes a long way. These are small but important gestures that support motivation and build a favorable work environment.

It has been proven that recognition and reward are the pillars of management success.

ACHIEVEMENT AND AFFILIATION NEEDS

An additional approach to motivation was detailed by a still another psychologist, **David McClelland.** His theory is somewhat similar to Maslow's and is also based on needs. In his book *The Achieving Society*, he presented what he called the "three dominate needs" theory. He identified them as achievement needs, affiliation needs, and the need for power.

McClelland believed that people have a strong need to set and accomplish goals and that they are willing to take some risks in achieving them. But they need to receive positive feedback while attempting and accomplishing them.

McClelland agreed with Maslow's assertion that some individuals want to be and need to be associated with a group and that this association provides them with individual motivation. Further, most people want to be liked and would rather cooperate than compete.

Further, at the highest stage in their development, people want to control situations and receive recognition. They desire reward and power. Quite often just the power to "decide" will fill this need.

Assuming that these thoughts have validity, the theory is that once you identify which needs a particular individual has, you can structure your management approach to address those needs.

You can accommodate those having achievement needs by assigning them difficult but not impossible projects. You encourage them by providing supportive feedback while the process is ongoing and positive recognition and reward at the project's termination, particularly so if it is successful.

For those recognized as the type of individual identified as having McClelland's affiliation needs, you can structure their tasks around group projects. Their working in a group motivates them to seek the approval of their fellow workers as well as that of management.

The success of groups is evident in society as a whole. Consider the accomplishments of veterans' organizations, the NRA, political parties, or even criminal gangs. Members of these groups all have a commonality of purpose and shared interests accompanied by, but not always evident to the members, the overpowering need to belong.

You can take advantage of this need in your agency. The affiliation individuals will do exceptionally well in narcotics or small investigative units, SWAT, or similar operations. Being a part of these types of groups fills this need. And again, people are rewarded by their belonging to the team and having pride in its success, and they will work hard to achieve it. For some, just being in the department fills the group-belonging need.

The power or control concept might best describe you. You do your best when placed in charge, and just the fact that you might be running things will in itself provide motivation. This level can be reached at any of the positions in supervision, management, or leadership that we are examining. Abraham Maslow called this level of accomplishment "self-actualization."

However, not all employees will promote or achieve a higher level in the organization. But both Maslow and McClelland identify the need of actualization or power. Simply put, being in charge and being looked up to and obeyed by others in the agency.

You can attempt to meet this need in your subordinates by assigning them to positions of responsibility and control in the various units that were discussed earlier. SWAT teams need leaders. So do other special-function units. An accident investigation team probably doesn't require a sergeant's supervision, but somebody has got to lead it. Maybe somebody with an actualization or power need could be assigned. Some officers who have particular interests or skills could fill that power need by being a gun guy, the range officer, or the one in charge at shooting training. Think about it—you are sure to come up with something. Then stand by and watch the results.

SOMEONE ONCE SAID:

Power is the ultimate aphrodisiac.
—*Henry Kissinger*

Also, notice that this kind of overlaps with the assertion that everybody needs or likes something. It is just another motivational method based on attempting to fill an individual's need or involving them in something that they are interested in.

About the same time that Abraham Maslow was developing his "needs" theory, another psychologist and author, **B. F. Skinner**, was also looking at motivation. While a professor at Harvard University, he developed a theory he termed "operant conditioning." He explained this developmental model in *Science and Human Behavior*.

Essentially, this concept demonstrated that behaviors that are reinforced are repeated. This translates into a management system that contains reinforcement and rewards, the proposition being that reinforced and rewarded behavior will be repeated.

This theory was based on what became known as the famous Skinner box experiments, where rats that inadvertently touched a bar in their cage were rewarded with cheese. They quickly learned that when they became hungry, by touching the bar they were rewarded with food.

Skinner's conclusions were that positive responses and behaviors can be obtained through repeated rewards.

This practice has always been engaged in by parents who promise rewards to encourage good behavior in their children. No one had used a formal approach to prove it before, but after Skinner's box experiments, it became an accepted management theory.

Even before Skinner, **Ivan Pavlov**, a Nobel Prize–winning Russian physiologist, with his dogs, developed what is now termed "classic conditioning." It is based on the same principle: pairing a neutral stimulus with a reward. Pavlov conditioned his dogs to respond to the signal of an audible metronome in order to receive a reward of food. Like Skinner's rats, Pavlov's dogs became conditioned to expect a reward if they performed a certain act. He documented these experiments in his book *Conditioned Reflexes*.

We probably shouldn't equate these animal experiments with our workers' behaviors, but a comparison does exist.

Management has learned the simple fact that rewarded behavior is repeated. And an expectation of reward does influence future positive behavior. And by fulfilling an employee's need for affiliation, recognition, and achievement, the resulting desired behavior is beneficial not only to the employee but to the organization.

Stephen R. Covey mentioned this while explaining the first habit in his best-selling book *The 7 Habits of Highly Effective People*. He termed it a stimulus/response theory, advising that through habit we are conditioned to respond in a particular way to a particular stimulus.

Although he put it differently, Covey agreed with Skinner and Pavlov that particular actions will result in identified and predicted responses and that management can elicit favorable behaviors from employees by providing the correct positive stimulus. These actions can become habit and a conditioned response. It is therefore imperative that the proper stimulus be provided to obtain the desired behavior.

From all of this we can accept that management has the ability to motivate its workers and can accomplish this in several ways as the noted experts have theorized. But basically it amounts to creating an organizational climate where the employee's needs are identified and met. If an employee knows that he or she will be rewarded and recognized for good performance, they can, as Covey noted, be conditioned and motivated to repeat the performance.

SOMEONE ONCE SAID:

**People work for money but go the extra mile
for recognition, praise and rewards.**
—Dale Carnegie

Unfortunately, a conditioned response can also result in a negative outcome.

ONCE UPON A TIME,
in a smaller department, the sergeant supervising the 4:00 p.m. to midnight shift would meet with his officers in a nearby bar for beer and pool at the conclusion of the shift a couple of times a week. Alcohol was consumed but not excessively so.

The city had been experiencing gang-related problems, and for that reason, officers were encouraged to wear concealable firearms off duty.

On one particular night, the sergeant and four officers were at the bar. A new bartender was speaking to one of the officers, wondering if the revolver that the owner kept near the cash register was adequate in case of an emergency. As he was showing it to the officer, another officer some distance away believed the bartender was pointing the gun at him. He drew his off-duty weapon and yelled "Drop it!"

Hearing the shout, the bartender turned toward the second officer, bringing the gun with him as he turned. Believing that he was now in danger, the second officer fired, seriously injuring the bartender.

The excuse given was that due to his training, the officer fired as a result of a "conditioned response" to having a gun pointed at him.

The officer was not criminally charged, but he, the sergeant, and the other officers were dealt with administratively.

This example, although not management related, does illustrate the validity of the conditioned response theory. The officer had been conditioned to the point that on observing the potential lethal danger, he reacted as he had been trained. Safety and survival, being the reward that was ingrained, resulted in the trained response.

JOB ENRICHMENT

SOMEONE ONCE SAID:

If you want people to do a good job, give them a good job to do—an enriched job.
—Frederick Herzberg

"Job enrichment" was a management approach promoted by **Frederick Herzberg**, another recognized clinical psychologist and author. Herzberg believed that by making the job more interesting and challenging, improved performance would result.

Through extensive interviewing of employees and determining what pleased them and what displeased them, he developed what he termed the theory of "hygiene and motivation." His findings somewhat parallel Maslow's hierarchy theory.

Herzberg identified the hygiene factors as lower-level needs that primarily serve to avoid pain and deprivation. They consist of pay and benefits, acceptable supervision, decent working conditions, status, and security.

In his book *Motivation to Work,* Herzberg described his belief that the hygiene factors are necessary for the employee to do the job; however, having them will not make the employee work harder or be more productive. Some of these factors may even be negative and cause dissatisfaction, such as an overbearing boss or too strict rules. Nevertheless, the employee will usually put up with them just to have the security of continued employment.

He termed the other set of needs as "motivators." These are the factors that not only allow the employees to work but encourage them to want to work harder.

Herzberg believed that examining the job itself and finding areas and/or ways in which to increase the importance and the responsibility of the worker would result in job satisfaction, performance, and psychological growth; hence, "job enrichment."

Sometimes the enrichment programs may not be actual but merely claimed to be so by the employer. There are examples where just a change of job title has served to create a sense of enrichment. Some departments have instituted a "corporal" rank between that of officer and sergeant. The newly created position's requirements and responsibilities may be insignificant or may not have changed at all. But just the title and the privilege of sewing a couple of stripes on the uniform are enough to provide the enrichment factor. Normally, no or only minimal remuneration is attached.

Unless it brings additional duties and increased responsibility, this type of imitation job enrichment should be avoided, as employees soon recognize it as a sham done by management just to assign a false sense of worth to some individuals.

SOMEONE ONCE SAID:

Justice will overtake fabricators of lies.
—Heraclitus

Not only will employees not become motivated through a false attempt at job enrichment if exposed as such, but management will suffer from what will surely be viewed as deceit.

This is not a wholesale indictment of all "corporal" or "officer in charge" or similar programs, but a caution to perhaps examine existing ones for validity and usefulness.

It is more desirable by far to actually engage in an actual enrichment program.

O. W. Wilson, the celebrated former superintendent of the Chicago Police Department, would have agreed wholeheartedly with the above assessment. In his book *Police Administration*, he devoted an entire chapter on the interpersonal and behavioral aspects of management.

He stressed the absolute necessity of moral and ethical behavior on the part of management to ensure loyalty of the followers. He urged that decisions affecting them be fair without hidden or unexplained motives behind them. Wilson warned that if any deceit on the part of the administration is uncovered or even perceived, the outcome will surely be a negative one.

Engaging in a job enrichment program is normally done at the departmental level, but in your position, you, too, can examine the role of your subordinates and search for enrichment possibilities.

One place to look for enriched duties is in *your* job description. Are you charged with any functions that might not need your authority to perform, even though they are important? If that is the case, you may want to determine whether a subordinate is capable of performing them. If so, consider delegating them.

If your agency is embarking on a new type of program, or if existing programs are short of resources, an identified enrichment possibility may already be at hand. Again, examine the time and expertise necessary to accomplish the tasks and consider assigning some of them to your line personnel if the tasks don't interfere with basic assigned responsibilities.

For example, if a particular type of crime is on the rise, assign an officer to develop a plan to combat it and then even have him or her become involved in or even lead a task force to implement the plan.

ONCE UPON A TIME,
in a middle-size city, car clouts and vehicle thefts became a continual problem in the parking area of a large shopping center. These were occurring mainly on the afternoon shift, arrests and clearances were nonexistent, and the area sergeant was exasperated and let the shift know it.

One of the beat officers tiring of taking the reports, mainly from tearful female shoppers, proposed to the sergeant that she and another officer be permitted to work a few hours undercover in the parking lot to see if they could alter the situation. She had studied the stats and identified the times and days of the week that were most problematic. The sergeant agreed, specifying, however, that it could only be done sporadically during the identified high-incidence periods and only if the shift was fat.

The plan was to use three officers, two undercover roving the lot and one in a marked unit patrolling nearby. When an incident occurred, that officer would respond to assist.

The strategy was highly successful, resulting in several arrests the first night in operation. It was later improved on by stationing an officer on the roof of the stores. This officer utilizing binoculars had an excellent view of the happenings below and could alert the officers below of observed criminal activity. Before long, after numerous arrests, the problem was practically eliminated. Additionally, the remaining officers on the shift all wanted to be involved. Some even volunteered to come in and work it on their days off without claiming overtime.

This is only a single example of how you can enrich the jobs of those working with you. If you've got a particular problem that needs a solution, you are encouraged to involve them, listen to them, pay attention to them, and reaffirm how important they are.

You will be surprised at the result!

Having someone assist you in scheduling or planning for special events is another suggestion you might use to enrich your subordinates' jobs.

A caution: do not give the employee busy work or responsibilities that are not at least a little challenging. This is termed "horizontal loading" or "job enlargement" and will not motivate the employee. It will more likely produce the opposite effect.

GIVING ATTENTION

SOMEONE ONCE SAID:

Since you cannot do good to all, you are to pay special attention to those who by the accidents of time, or place, or circumstances, are brought into closer connection with you.

—Saint Augustine

Oftentimes, because the law enforcement profession itself is challenging and rewarding, motivational and job enrichment programs do not have to be formal or require significant change to get results.

Coming to us from the period of industrialization, another usable and still valid management theory was discovered. Actually, by accident.

During that period many workers labored in factory jobs that quickly grew boring and tedious. As this occurred, production suffered. In an effort to increase output, management examined working conditions to see what effect they might have on performance.

In an Illinois Hawthorne Western Electric factory, a study in lighting was conducted, the thought being that perhaps the workers couldn't see well enough to perform their required assembling of parts tasks. Management gradually increased the light level in one part of the factory, leaving it static in the rest of the workplace. Upon each lighting increase, production also increased. Then to test the accuracy of the experiment, management did the reverse by incrementally dimming the lights in another test area. Surprisingly, again at each change, production increased. Even when the lighting was reduced to near darkness, the effect was the same—more production. Management then experimented with other changes. Break times were adjusted by time of day and length. Shift start times were altered, the workday was shortened, and so on. Again, each modification resulted in an increase in output.

Elton Mayo, the industrial researcher who conducted the studies, discovered that it was not the changes in physical working conditions that brought about the performance improvements. It was that the employees realized that management was taking an interest in them, and they reacted to the attention by working harder. This phenomena has been termed the "Hawthorne effect."

Modern management gurus have accepted that the Hawthorne effect is valid and have encouraged organizations to adopt it. Not the unnecessary changing of working conditions, but the increasing of the attention paid to the employees and their work conditions.

At the first supervisory level, you most likely don't have the ability to substantially alter working conditions, but you certainly have the ability, actually the responsibility, to pay attention to the workers. This attention can be directed at the individual or at a group or shift. It can be accomplished as previously noted, by engaging in ride-a-longs, identifying particular problems on their beat or shift, and challenging them to attempt solutions.

SOMEONE ONCE SAID:

When we focus on others, our world expands.
—Daniel Coleman

FLEXIBILITY VERSUS CONSISTENCY

It has been preached that flexibility is a requirement for a successful supervisor. You must be able to act and react to a variety of situations in a variety of ways. This includes how you interact with your subordinates.

A flexible approach to employees for a supervisor is one where an effort is made to accommodate their personal styles and needs within policy but still get the job done.

Flexibility can be applied to individual officers and situations. But be warned, care must be taken so that a double standard isn't created. In other words, you can be flexible, but you must avoid any hint of favoritism.

A recruit fresh out of the academy or an officer transferring into a new and strange patrol area should be handled differently than an officer with a decade of local experience. The newcomers of course need closer supervision and more instruction than the old veteran. This may be viewed by some as preferential treatment, but an explainable and reasonable purpose for the different handling of individuals can be acceptable.

Once upon a time,

a sheriff's department had a regulation that required that anytime a patrol deputy left his or her assigned beat that both dispatch and the shift sergeant be notified via radio. This was done so that the supervisor, dispatch, and adjoining beat officers would be aware of the fact and could provide service in that beat area if necessary. The requirement was in place no matter what caused the deputy to leave the beat, whether transporting to jail or court, providing backup in adjoining beats, and so on.

During the 4:00 p.m. to midnight shift, radio traffic, just through normal activity, became excessive, and because of this, most deputies ignored the practice of making the required "off-the-beat" notifications via the radio. Supervisors knew of this and overlooked it, although a technical rule violation.

However, probationary deputies, "newbies," were required to make off-the-beat notifications as part of their break-in and learning process.

At briefing one afternoon, a sergeant was questioned as to why this was, and the response given was "'Cause you got to learn the rules before you start breaking them!"

The sergeant was practicing one of **Sun Tzu's** philosophies as stated in his writing, *The Art of War*. "A new soldier must be treated with humanity, but kept under control by means of iron discipline."

A short time later, a newly hired deputy, who was having serious problems with most aspects of becoming a patrol officer, was rejected during probation. One factor was an apparent disregard for following orders.

The probationary deputy fought the separation, and a hearing was scheduled, at which noncompliance with the off-the-beat rule and the supervisor's ignoring it for most deputies were brought up.

The argument was made that petty rules such as the off-the-beat notifications were knowingly violated by deputies without consequence and with tacit approval from supervisors, and the probationer was just following the practice.

Management argued that in a dynamic environment of emergency operations, a certain amount of "flexibility" was given to supervisors in order to make things work. But the probationary employees were not permitted this leniency during the training phase of their employment. The judge agreed, and the department won.

After all was said and done, the department modified the directive about radio off-the-beat notifications, requiring only that when leaving their assigned beat, officers should make an entry in their computer log.

The point here is that there does exist the need for some flexibility in an operation, in both organizational and individual handling of personnel. This provides supervisors and subordinates with greater latitude on how they do their job.

In general, law enforcement officers are permitted much discretion because no set of laws or regulations can prescribe what to do in every situation. The possibilities are too numerous to have a rule for every circumstance that may be encountered.

Most employees respond affirmatively to a more hands-off type of management that gives them some latitude in deciding how some things are done. It normally falls to the first-line supervisor to establish these "flexible" parameters.

If employees are trained and proficient at their job, they shouldn't need constant oversight and correction. And for the most part, they certainly appreciate more freedom in their day-to-day performance. If they do innovate in some areas and are successful, notice of the fact should be made.

This follows the previously cited authorities' beliefs that employees seek recognition and reward, which if given, will benefit the organization.

But unfortunately, in almost every group, there are some who require more direct supervision and, if given their choice of functioning, will pick the path of least effort and least productivity. This is where the other side of your supervisory flexibility comes in. In these cases, rather than granting less oversight, you may have to provide closer supervision and additional direction.

Once you identify these employees, you can then tailor a corrective approach to their situation.

Are they just not working hard because of laziness or lost interest, or are they having trouble because of lack of knowledge or ability? In either case, some action on your part is necessary.

It is not unusual for officers to lose enthusiasm for the job. The newness and excitement are gone, and after a while, one call is pretty much the same as those handled in the past. Also, because policing is currently an environment in constant change, some may have quit trying to keep up.

Still others might be having personal off-the-job problems such as financial difficulties, divorce, and so on. There is normally little you can do to help them correct their personal issues other than express sympathy and perhaps recommend professional help.

No matter their cause, on-the-job problems should be discussed and solutions sought.

The key is to be flexible in your approach. Remember, people are different, and the problems they have will be different too. What may work in once instance or with one individual will not work in every case. You must make an effort to determine what the problem is and then tailor a solution. Sometimes just an urging to "get your butt in gear" is all it will take. In other cases, training, counseling, or maybe sterner disciplinary actions may be necessary.

On the other hand . . .

SOMEONE ONCE SAID:

Consistency is the foundation of virtue.
—Francis Bacon

Flexibility is important, but consistency is also an essential quality in the supervision of others.

Rules and regulations exist in order to establish and maintain correct and standardized operations, and consistency in their application cannot be totally overlooked.

For people to be able to work for you and with you, they must have some idea about your views and expectations, and these must generally be consistent.

In addition to your own consistent response to situations, your subordinates should be able to expect and receive similar management responses and approaches from your peers. Your supervisory styles may be different, but all first-line supervisors should be fairly uniform in day-to-day operations.

If this is not the case, your subordinates may be confused about what is acceptable or unacceptable behavior. This confusion may lead to problems.

ONCE UPON A TIME,
in a medium-size department, two sergeants were assigned to the graveyard shift. Both of these sergeants supervised the same officers on a rotating basis.

One of the sergeants, if categorized, would certainly be classified as an autocratic supervisor. He had rules, and they had better not be broken. Any slight deviation from his directives would incur his wrath.

The other sergeant was more laid-back, and as long as things didn't completely fall apart during his shift, he was happy.

The first sergeant had an ironclad rule that officers were not to take their entitled breaks during the first or last hour of the shift. It was his belief that if they went on break at the beginning of the shift, their start to workday would be greatly delayed, and if they took their break near the end of shift, they would be ending their workday early.

The officers knew this rule, but the other sergeant didn't. He had no such concerns.

> One night, two officers not remembering which sergeant was on took their break during the last hour of the shift.
>
> Sergeant number one was waiting for them when they returned to the office. He had prepared a written reprimand for them both, for failure to obey a directive.
>
> Knowing that this negative document in their personnel files could hurt their promotional chances, the officers were upset and filed a grievance against the sergeant through their union.
>
> They didn't contest the rule, just the two sergeants' inconsistency of applying it.
>
> The department didn't rescind the reprimand and the grievance went to arbitration, which the union won.
>
> The arbitration judge found that "such inconsistency of supervisory practices was a management, not an employee problem" and ruled in the officers' favor.
>
> The whole affair greatly upset the department head, as it made his administration look bad for such a petty incident to end with a negative outcome for management.

Clearly, the problem was that management was unaware of the inconsistency in supervision at the working level. The sergeants sharing supervision over the same shift of officers should have coordinated their expectations and methods more closely to eliminate obvious conflicts.

SOMEONE ONCE SAID:

What we have here is a failure to communicate.
—*Cool Hand Luke*

If you should become aware that you and your fellow supervisors are applying different and contradictory directives or instructions to your subordinates, it is your responsibility to clear up these discrepancies and avoid outright conflicts in procedures.

Communicate with your peers. Consistency in operations is a must, for it is the necessary element that keeps an agency moving in the same direction. When one of your subordinates, in response to a directive, says, "OK, but Sergeant So-and-So said to do it this way," it is time to contact that sergeant and get on the same page.

This seems to counter what has been said about employing flexibility in your approach to working with your subordinates.

The difference is that flexibility is the tool in your management style that is not rigid and permits various strategies and methodologies to be used. It is an approach that is utilized individually, normally for decision making or problem solving. This individual flexibility permits consideration of different approaches in either similar or different situations to achieve desired results. But, again, it mustn't be at odds with the practices of your peers. If different styles or approaches clash, they must be resolved at your level. You should also be aware that officers will often "shop" for answers from their various supervisors, and when answers differ, they will follow the most desirable alternative or path of least resistance.

All this being said, there is one area in which consistency is an absolute requisite! That is officer safety! It is imperative that all agency supervisors, managers, and leaders insist that correct tactics and procedures involving officer safety be followed exactly as they are taught. Individual preferences cannot be tolerated in this critical area of operations.

MISTAKES AND FAILURES

As time goes by, being human, you will certainly make mistakes. This is part of the learning process, and a normal part of the job, provided that you learn from these mistakes.

The belief is that if you do something that is terribly wrong, it will quickly become apparent and be pointed out to you. And once you realize the error, you will hopefully not repeat it. This is a painful but proven way to learn and gain experience.

Also, once your mistake becomes public, don't try to justify or excuse it, as this only extends the discussion of it. You should make a short explanation of why you committed the error, if reasonable, and then drop it there. An initial admission, simply stated, will normally deter a lengthy rehashing of the incident and preclude a prolonged discussion.

According to another theory, if you are observant, you don't have to make all of the mistakes yourself. By watching others and paying attention to their mistakes, you can learn from them and avoid making the same mistakes.

> ### ONCE UPON A TIME,
> at a shift briefing, the supervisor conducting it chewed out the entire group of officers present. Apparently, a couple of officers had been overheard planning to meet for coffee on the radio. This greatly incensed the shift supervisor. The entire shift, being a captive audience, received the same loud complaint about how unprofessional it must seem to citizens monitoring on radio scanners when they heard police officers planning a break on the air! And if it occurred again, punitive action would follow! Each officer was then directed to review the department's radio procedures policy prior to hitting the streets.
>
> In the parking lot after the briefing, most of the shift gathered to discuss what a mean SOB the supervisor was for making such a big deal about such a small thing! And for taking on the entire shift for the actions of a couple of individuals! All agreed this was an issue that should have been handled in private with the guilty individuals! Additionally, the two perpetrators were not pleased about their being reprimanded in front of all the others either.
>
> Needless to say, the sergeant lost a great deal of respect from the officers on that shift. Everyone in the group decided that if they ever became a supervisor, that they would *not* make a similar mistake.

Like these officers, you, too, can learn from someone else's mistakes simply by observing. The entire shift learned that it is unwise to shotgun the group with criticisms and accusations, unless the misconduct applies to all of them. The individuals involved should have been singled out and dealt with privately.

SOMEONE ONCE SAID:

**It's good to learn from your mistakes. It's
better to learn from other people's mistakes.**
—Warren Buffett

Unfortunately, some individuals, after making a mistake, or perhaps a series of them, can develop a self-destructive attitude. They may get down on themselves and begin to believe that they are a failure. This can happen when they are new to a position, with new responsibilities, and receive little positive reinforcement or the opposite, an adverse performance review. This depression often leads to even more mistakes and a deleterious mind-set deepens.

In this state these people lose confidence and are often reluctant or afraid to make a decision or take even a small risk or chance. Or they start to believe that no matter what they do, it will be wrong, and they will become indifferent about their job. Continuing this downward spiral can affect not only their career but their entire life.

In the 1960s, **Dr. Maxwell Maltz**, a plastic surgeon, noted that many of his patients came to him for unnecessary improvement, not because they really needed it, but because they had a poor self-image. In many cases, their problem was psychological, not physical. They were often unhappy, insecure, uncertain, and lonely and they placed the blame on their looks. By studying these cases from a psychological perspective, he determined that the patients often had a poor mental self-image. This resulted from a perception of failure, caused by making and remaking mistakes. He believed that an individual's brain is influenced by the thoughts and images sent to it. If these are negative, a negative attitude results.

Maltz described his thoughts in a best-selling book *Psycho-Cybernetics*. In it he explained that our self-image is the cornerstone of our mental state and influences the way we live. How we view our successes and failures, actual or perceived, defines us.

Maltz wrote that if we permit our mistakes and other negatives to determine who or what we "think" we are, we will adopt that attitude and actually believe it. And if those thoughts describe us as unworthy or a failure, that is what we are likely to become.

The truth is, even if you have made some past mistakes and failed to accomplish what you desired, you should consider these mistakes as educational steps and lessons learned. The psycho-cybernetics theory states that our brains do not distinguish between imagination and reality. The brain acts based on information sent to it by our thoughts. So if we can think positively about events, imperfect though they might have been, we can create a new paradigm of success, happiness, fulfillment, and self-confidence.

SOMEONE ONCE SAID:

Once you replace negative thoughts with positive ones, you'll start having positive results.
—*Willie Nelson*

Dr. Norman Vincent Peale espoused similar thoughts in his celebrated book *The Power of Positive Thinking*. Even though his work is strongly linked to faith and gospel teachings, it, too, outlined methods to succeed through visualization and creating a peaceful mind. "People must let go of worry and negative thoughts and replace them with beliefs of success and positive outcomes," he wrote, asserting that the mind controls how an individual believes and that most obstacles are mental in nature.

Simply put, both authors encourage individuals to attempt to always look on the bright side and don't let mistakes rule your outlook. Even though it was not obvious to you, most likely something positive resulted from whatever happened.

SOMEONE ONCE SAID:

I've not failed 10,000 times. I've not failed once. I've succeeded in proving that those 10,000 ways won't work
—*Thomas Edison*

To adopt this positive approach will take work. One suggested method is through what is termed "visualization." This is a process of positively imagining the future success of the venture, then determining how to achieve it. This belief in a positive outcome will go a long ways toward making success happen. This is a simple explanation of Dr. Peale's teachings about the power of positive thinking.

The theory of management by objectives or setting goals to reach an objective will be discussed later. That same process can be utilized in self-image improvement.

SOMEONE ONCE SAID:

Forget mistakes, forget failure, forget everything except what you're going to do now, and do it.
—*Will Durant*

These same principles apply to your interaction with and supervision of others as well. If you observe them descending into the failure mode, do what you can to assist them. Their depression may not be job related, but as a good supervisor, it is your responsibility to look into their problem and offer assistance. Whatever is troubling them may be of a serious, and they may be approaching a desperate level. If you cannot assist them, it is your responsibility to get them some type of help. There are far too many suicides in the law enforcement profession. Recent statistics indicate that the number of officers taking their own lives is equal to the number of officers being killed in the line of duty.

Both numbers must be reduced!

DECISION MAKING AND RISK TAKING

SOMEONE ONCE SAID:

**Decisiveness is the one word that
makes a good manager.**
—Lee Iacocca

As a first-line supervisor, you will be constantly called on to make decisions. They will be of all types, ranging from petty to highly consequential. For example, at a shift beginning a troop may approach you with: "Hey Sarge, my car won't start, what should I do?" The answer is relatively simple: either "Take another one" or "Get this one running." Fairly simple to you but meaningful to the requester. Either he or she really didn't know what to do or just didn't want to take the responsibility of deciding.

Sometimes these situations will give you the opportunity to apply McGregor's Theory Y approach to involving subordinates in the problem-solving and decision-making process.

If it is an individual problem, you can include the subordinate in the decision making by simply asking, "What do you think?" or "Do you have any ideas?" Now they are involved. And you might be surprised at their proposed solution.

If the concern involves more than one person, again, you can decide it yourself or maybe hold a group discussion. If the problem is an important one, solve it more formally, through the use of a committee. Or it might require a decision from on high, but it is your decision initially on how a problem should be handled.

You will occasionally be involved in more serious decisions that come up in emergencies, such as whether or not to let a pursuit continue, whether an incident justifies a SWAT response, and so on.

Comprehensive advice cannot be given on each situation that requires you to decide. But you must be prepared to make decisions. Try to anticipate the type of an emergency that might arise in your jurisdiction and predetermine what should be done to resolve it.

You can prepare yourself by being knowledgeable of your department's special and general orders, most of which were developed in anticipation of or as a result of some type of past emergency.

Specialty training courses have also examined the many types of emergencies that occur and have developed appropriate responses. Even if you have not had the opportunity to attend the training, try to pick the brain of someone who has. Or you can read up on the subject yourself. There is instructional material covering almost every type of incident online. OSHA and www.ready.gov are good informational sources.

Also, don't be afraid to ask. Through social media, both official and personal, you can no doubt obtain information that can help you.

SOMEONE ONCE SAID:

I think this life is hard
without assistance from others.
—RuPaul

It takes some humility, and it might be a jolt to your ego to admit that you don't know something. But not to seek help and subsequently make a critical mistake is much worse, for the successful resolution of both the incident and your future.

Just believe that when something critical occurs, it now may well be your responsibility to make the proper decisions. And these incidents do occur.

SOMEONE ONCE SAID:

It's not about making the right choice, it's about making a choice and making it right.
—J. R. Rim

Decision making has been identified as one of the critical abilities of a successful supervisor, manager, and leader. So if you can develop the skill of making a proper assessment of a problem that requires action and then taking the correct action, you have gone a long way toward assuring your future.

President Abraham Lincoln developed a system to assist him in making decisions. He appointed cabinet members who were not always supportive of him, and then he sought their advice on tough decisions. This way he got several sides of the arguments and a variety of possible solutions. This quite often expanded his alternatives and gave him options that he may not have considered. It also provided him with support from those who initially suggested or agreed with the course of action he ended up taking.

You, unfortunately, do not have a cadre of handpicked assistants to offer you guidance, but quite often there will be people willing to offer advice and assistance. These are your own officers, other law enforcement agency personnel, fire or rescue personnel, and citizens who may have particular knowledge such as medical professionals. Many times witnesses and neighbors possess knowledge that you do not. Don't be afraid to solicit and use what assistance is available. Those stripes didn't give you absolute knowledge on how to deal with every contingency. And now that you are in a supervisory position, when you make a decision, it is important to be correct most of the time. Valid or not, being correct is judged as being competent, and the reverse is also true.

It follows then that being right and making the correct decisions are important. Sometimes at this level, it is more than important, it is critical.

When we do right, nobody remembers.
When we do wrong, nobody forgets.
—*Hells Angels Motorcycle Club*

Most times making a decision is relatively simple. As noted, there are laws, past procedures, general orders, and so on to assist you. You also have your own knowledge and experience to guide you. But sometimes the answers might be ambiguous or you draw a total blank on what to do.

This is where risk taking comes in.

Risk comes from not knowing
what you're doing.
—*Warren Buffett*

Dozens of books have been written on decision making and just as many theories have been proffered on how to go about it. The "rational choice" theory is one of these. Rational decisions are consistently made based on what is the best perceived outcome or resultant situation for persons involved. An irrational decision is one made when the circumstances or facts surrounding it are not correct or different from what is believed. Sometimes, though, the irrational decision can be the correct one.

> **ONCE UPON A TIME,**
> a state trooper made a stop on a suspected DUI driver. All of the objective signs were there: poor balance, slurred speech, jittery and emotionally anxious appearance, and so on. However, no odor of alcohol was present. The officer then suspected drugs, but the driver was a local clergyman, so the officer was skeptical of drug use. The driver apologized, stating that he had been attending a dying parishioner and was fatigued. The officer had

noted slight damage to the right side of the car, but the driver explained it away, stating that it had been scraped while parked at a shopping center. Not sure how to proceed, the officer called his supervisor.

After arriving on the scene and listening to the officer's explanation, the sergeant had to decide what to do as the officer was clearly at a loss. Something was wrong but what? The simplest thing to do was to release the pastor. He had made it this far, was a short distance from his home, and could probably make it. Or they could park his car and obtain transportation for him or drive him home themselves. Or as they had probable cause, they could arrest and chemically test him.

Because the sergeant had an uneasy, perhaps irrational feeling, he had the officer arrest the pastor.

While at the local hospital where the chemical tests were completed, the sergeant encountered an officer from the local police department just leaving the emergency room. It seems that approximately an hour before, a child riding a bicycle had been struck by an automobile in a hit-and-run accident. The child was in critical condition.

By comparing times and location and the damage to the pastor's car, the sergeant determined that the clergyman arrested by the trooper was the driver involved in the collision. The blood test indicated a significant amount of a prescribed opiate in his system.

Many would judge that the sergeant had made an unwise or irrational decision to arrest the pastor. However, in this case, it proved to be a correct one. The point is that even if most facts indicate that a rational course of action be taken, sometimes a risk needs to be taken. Had the "rational choice" doctrine been followed, a miscarriage of justice would have occurred.

Actually, that is the wrong question to ask. Inspector Callahan was incorrect. Luck has nothing to do with deciding a course of action.

Decision making is one of the most important areas of supervision, so even though it is repetitious, you should consider the following list of possible actions to take when you have to make a decision but don't have any idea of what to do. The steps below may help you reduce the risk of making an incorrect decision:

1. Think intensively about the problem. Gather all the information you can about it, and have a burning desire to solve it.
2. Like Lincoln, ask someone. There are no doubt numerous people who will have a ready and correct answer for you. They may have faced a similar situation or just be more experienced. As noted previously, don't be ashamed to ask subordinates or citizens; their knowledge may surprise you. Remember, though, they are only advising; the decision and its results are yours.
3. Examine and consider alternatives. Sometimes they are not apparent, and you will have to utilize reason, imagination, and other objective appraisals to sort them out and come up with an acceptable and workable solution.
4. Balance risk and result. Weigh the best and worst outcomes of each proposal and then decide.
5. Consider the effect of delay, which would allow you to gather more information. It has been stated, however, that a good decision not made on time is a bad decision.
6. Do not, not decide. Doing nothing is the worst thing you can do!

As time goes by and you gain experience your risks will become less formidable because you most likely will have encountered similar dilemmas, acted on them, and learned from them.

SOMEONE ONCE SAID:

Take calculated risks.
That is quite different from being rash.
—*General George S. Patton*

Sometimes taking a risk will not be the appropriate course. Sometimes risks can be avoided by heeding advice.

ONCE UPON A TIME,
a newly promoted sergeant was assigned to the traffic division in a larger department. Other than traffic situations occasionally encountered on beat patrol, the new supervisor had no real experience in traffic control or management.

One evening, just at dark, a big rig ran off the freeway, went up a steep shoulder bank, and overturned. It was towing a trailer loaded with steel bars that came to rest on its side, blocking the shoulder and part of the slow lane. Miraculously, the binders held. The load stayed together and was still attached to the trailer.

Removal of the loaded trailer that night would cause a several-hour closure of the freeway and diversion of traffic onto surface streets. This would, in turn, require substantial traffic control on the created detour. The sergeant could imagine the overtime that would be expended, plus the likelihood of minor accidents caused by detouring all of the freeway traffic onto the surface streets. Perhaps in daylight the removal could be accomplished without totally closing down the freeway.

One of the officers assigned to work the crash had eleven years' experience in the traffic division, and she cautioned the sergeant that it would be too dangerous to leave the trailer in place.

The sergeant overruled the officer and directed the highway department to "cone off" the slow lane with flares and reflective cones.

> Several hours after officers cleared the scene, a vehicle plowed through the cones and struck the overturned trailer. Three people in the vehicle were killed.
>
> Culpability was reduced substantially because the vehicle was traveling at an extremely high rate of speed and the driver was under the influence of alcohol at the time of the crash. Yet some responsibility was placed on the department and the city.

Again, rank doesn't always make you right. When taking a risk, try to utilize all available information. Even though the sergeant's rationale had merit, the seasoned officer's advice should have probably prevailed.

SOMEONE ONCE SAID:

Many receive advice, but few profit from it.
—Publilius Syrus

In his work "A Constitutional Model of Leadership," **Alfred DeCrane Jr.** listed the qualities that the drafters of the Constitution believed were necessary to establish a framework for governance. One of the primary qualities was self-confidence. He believed that self-confidence was necessary for leaders to possess in order to take on challenges and to enable prudent risk taking.

Like those of the framers, the risks you take are proportionate to your self-confidence. As you are exposed to more situations and gather experience your self-confidence will grow and risk taking will diminish. But do not become overconfident to the point that your developed decision-making skill suffers.

SOMEONE ONCE SAID:

**Ponder and deliberate before you
make a move.**
—Sun Tzu

BE A ROLE MODEL

Because you are an officer, your appearance, demeanor, and general obedience to the rules were observed by the public and your supervisors alike. If you were not looking or behaving according to expectations, you most likely were notified and perhaps corrective action was taken. This same form of observation will accompany you as you move up through the ranks, but with one major difference. Now how you look and behave will also be noticed by those you supervise. And your actions have an effect on them. Hopefully, an affirmative one. Some may even admire you and want to be like you. That's great! You can be and should be a role model. A positive one!

In your supervisory position, the way you conduct yourself and do your job impacts not only you but your subordinates. Just as you expect those working for you to obey the rules, you, like them, must also follow the rules.

ONCE UPON A TIME,

an officer made a routine stop of a suspected DUI. He detected the odor of alcohol, got the lone driver out, conducted the balance and Breathalyzer tests, and determined that the driver was under the influence. The driver was then placed under arrest. So far, a routine, well-conducted, and by-the-book traffic stop.

During the handcuffing, the suspect resisted, broke way, and assumed a karate-type stance. The officer, taking no chances, pulled the baton and struck the subject three or four times, aiming first at the arms and shoulders and then at the legs to take the subject down. It worked.

Once on the ground, the subject was handcuffed. It all went quickly and smoothly. So smoothly that the officer did not charge the driver with resisting arrest. The suspect did not appear injured and was taken straight to jail. No notation about the baton use was made in the arrest report. However, the incident had been recorded on the officer's body-worn camera (BWC).

At the end of the shift the supervisor reviewed and approved the arrest report. The supervisor did not review the officer's BWC recording, even though such a review was required by departmental policy on all physical arrests.

Five months later the city was served with a civil suit claiming that the officer had brutalized the citizen. During the arrest he had suffered a fractured collar bone and a mild concussion and was experiencing memory loss. These were alleged to have resulted from the officers unneccesary use of the club.

The department conducted an investigation, concluding that the arrest was valid. But after a review of the BWC recording, it was also learned that a baton had been used and a couple of the baton strokes, although probably unintended, had struck the citizen in the neck and head area. The administration also discovered that the use of the baton had not been included in the report and, further, that the supervisor had not reviewed the body cam recording as required.

The individual's attorney subpoenaed the recording and argued that the clubbing constituted brutality, not simply overcoming mild resistance. Also noted was the fact that the citizen was not charged with resisting arrest or assaulting an officer. Further noted was that the department should have been aware of the beating, as it was clearly evident in the recording, and that the department was hiding that fact.

The DUI charge was dropped, and the city settled the lawsuit with a substantial payoff to the citizen.

Both the arresting officer and his supervisor were formally disciplined. The belief was that the inclusion of the baton use in the arrest report and the required review of the recording at the time could have alerted the department to the possibility of injury, or claimed injury, and that appropriate follow-up could have been made. Also, the charge of an attempted cover-up could have been avoided.

The supervisor compounded the problem by publicly blaming the officer for not bringing the fact that he had used the baton and injured the arrestee to his attention, overlooking his own complicity by not reviewing the video. This led to mistrust from his other subordinates, in addition to that already expressed by his superiors.

Again, the lesson to be learned: your actions, or inactions in this case, can result in problems, not only for you but others. If you expect your subordinates to act correctly, you must do the same.

SOMEONE ONCE SAID:

No man is fit to command another that cannot command himself.
—*William Penn*

If your actions and demeanor are not correct or positive, they can have an adverse effect on your interaction with subordinates and it can be a costly one.

If they see that you are not paying strict attention to the rules, they may figure, why should they? The same goes for your work effort. If you appear to be exerting less than expected interest or energy, why then should they?

As can be imagined, the results will be detrimental. Not only might subordinates copy your habits and become a supervisory problem, it will be your supervisory problem!

It is difficult to hold them to conduct or performance standards that you do not demonstrate. So, it is certainly in your and the department's best interests to set a good example and be a positive role model.

SOMEONE ONCE SAID:

**What you do has far greater impact
than what you say.**
—Stephen Covey

FINALLY

If an organization is to operate efficiently and get the most out of its employees, it is imperative that the first-line supervisors be competent and capable. It is believed by many that this level, because of its continual direct contact with the actual workers, is the most important in an organization. It all begins here.

SOMEONE ONCE SAID:

Do what's right.
Do the best you can.
Treat others like you want to be treated.
—Lou Holtz

MANAGEMENT

Congratulations! Another step or so up the ladder. In most agencies, this would be to a position of lieutenant, captain, or similar.

Again, the benefits are obvious: more pay, generally working in an office and off the road, fewer night shifts, and, for the most part, weekends and holidays off.

These certainly are benefits, but there are some drawbacks. Perhaps the greatest drawback is that you are now one step further away from the actual job and career that you signed up for. In most cases, administration is your responsibility. Paperwork instead of chasing bad guys. Making reports instead of making arrests.

Providing coordination between the workers and the "brass" is now one of your main responsibilities.

In this position your duties will most likely involve supervising programs more than people. But people are still an important factor in your job.

You will continue to work with both the command levels above and the supervisory levels below you. But as noted, in this position, you most likely will not be directly involved in supervising day-to-day operations, but you will be charged with carrying out the objectives of the organization and meeting the goals established by executive management.

TRAINING AND LEARNING

The transition to managing or being a part of managing a departmental field district or program area is perhaps the easiest change to make, for in most cases you will be overseeing basically the same functions that you were previously engaged in, only at a different level. Now you will be supervising the supervisors. The rules, responsibilities, and organizational goals that you have been working with remain the same. Also, the management philosophies have probably not changed.

If, on the other hand, you are placed in charge of a particular segment of the organization, either a geographical district or a staff unit that has a specialized function and responsibility, you must make every effort to learn and master the particular skills and knowledge that this specialized assignment requires.

This type of assignment might be in the personnel area such as hiring, training, internal affairs, and so on. Some departments charge middle management with the tasks of planning, budgeting, or data processing. Or it might be a unique criminal investigations function, such as narcotics, gang enforcement, or a fraud or traffic unit. In many cases, this may constitute almost an entire career change. If so, you are essentially starting over.

SOMEONE ONCE SAID:

People advance to their level of incompetence.
—Laurence J. Peter

That was said by respected author **Laurence J. Peter** and was the thesis of his celebrated book *The Peter Principle*. Unfortunately, this is sometimes a factual condition, and it is a problem. His point was that if you are proficient in your current position, you will be promoted, and you will continue to be promoted until you reach a level or position where you are not capable of performing, having reached your level of incompetence.

But it doesn't have to be! You had to have been a successful supervisor to have been promoted. You acquired the knowledge of the job and the supervisory skills to have performed at a reasonably high and competent level. Thus, you earned advancement.

Now, however, that job knowledge you gained through experience and training may not be applicable or sufficient for your new position.

In most organizations people are not promoted to jobs that they are clearly incapable of performing. That being the case, you have demonstrated the ability to acquire the knowledge to do this job! It is now your responsibility to do so.

This is normally accomplished through experience and training. Experience will take care of itself, providing you have an open and observing mind and learn from what's going on around you.

Training can be either formal or informal. Quite often, upon promotion, your department can and will send you to specialized training that introduces you to your new responsibilities and instructs you on them.

The FBI National Academy offers one of the best courses for middle managers. Check to see if the training is offered in your area. Other than your position being vacant for about three months, there is no cost for this training.

Any formal training is beneficial, and you should take advantage of it if possible. Most junior colleges offer management training, and you should sign up for some courses if available. If none are offered locally, the internet is another source to consider. There are numerous programs available, both online and virtual, including www.johnmaxwell.co and www.devry.edu, to name just two.

Sometimes, however, you will be left to learn by what is termed "OJT," or on-the-job training. If this is the case, the responsibility will be on you to learn for the most part on your own.

Oftentimes you can do this by skillfully questioning the person who formerly had the job, or by contacting people holding similar positions either in your agency or in other agencies.

SOMEONE ONCE SAID:

Listen! When you talk, you only say something that you already know; when you listen you might learn what someone else knows.
—Dalai Lama

As noted, the basic concepts and principles of management are universal; locations, situations, and participants change, but the basics do not.

For example, at the supervisory level, it is also important to know your people. This may be even more important at this stage of your career. At the mid-management level you have a greater opportunity to enrich their jobs by creating special programs, and if you know their skills and interests, you can better find the right person for the job.

SOMEONE ONCE SAID:

A man learns in two ways, one by reading, and the other by association with smarter people.
—Will Rogers

If possible, try to surround yourself with people who know more about subjects or functions that you might be weak in.

This includes your subordinates. If they have experience in the unit, you can learn from them. They will be flattered and impressed by your attention and asking them for assistance.

**Sometimes it is better to ask some questions
than it is to know all the answers.**
—James Thurber

It will soon become obvious what technical knowledge you lack. Many times you simply won't know the answer to simple questions, or there are certain areas where you consistently delay making decisions. Not because the decisions are particularly difficult, but because you may lack the information to correctly make them. If this becomes too regular of an occurrence, you may be validating Dr. Peter's principle.

This is where you must depend on others for assistance. It may be personally embarrassing to admit that you don't know something, but it is better to ask than to make a critical error by making a hasty and wrong decision. Hopefully, when you need it, they'll "have your six."

**It takes twenty years to build a reputation,
and five minutes to ruin it.**
—Warren Buffett

Being right at least most of the time is very important.

If you have access to it, the internet currently is one of the best resources available. It can provide the answers to most technical questions. Your departmental manuals can also provide guidance. Again, don't be afraid to ask. If you don't know something, there is probably someone around who does.

**The best thing I did was to choose
the right heroes.**
—Warren Buffett

Another form of learning and furthering your development at this stage in your career might be to select a mentor. In every organization there are individuals who are recognized as possessing job and common knowledge that kind of sets them apart and who seem destined to go all the way to the top. They appear to possess those qualities that make them not only effective employees but effective instructors and leaders. This is the type of person to select as an advisor or mentor.

SOMEONE ONCE SAID:

Taking charge of your own learning is a part of taking charge of your life.
—Warren G. Bennis

Having a mentor to watch and learn positive skills from is certainly desirable.

And as pointed out earlier, you can learn from negative sources and experiences as well. Not only can you learn from your mistakes, but by being observant and watching others when they err, you can advance your education through their slipups.

MODERN MANAGEMENT

Once you have acquainted yourself with your basic responsibilities and have settled into your position as a middle manager, it is time now to start functioning and to make things work. It is now that you must make the transition from supervisor to manager and hopefully from manager to leader.

When we examine the processes of middle management, it is important to look at the works of a French mining engineer named **Henri Fayol**. He set forth a concept of administration now called "Fayolism."

Even though completed in the latter part of the nineteenth century but published in 1916, his work *General and Industrial Management* was one of the first comprehensive looks at the theory of modern management, and it remains applicable and valuable today.

Management processes were certainly in place prior to Fayol's cataloguing them, such as tribalism, monarchies, or those utilized in military organizations. But none were as complete and contained all of the elements now deemed essential for modern management.

Fayol believed that organizational administration was a subject of extreme and universal importance and that it was an area of institutional behavior that must be studied, modified if necessary, and, if correct, implemented.

Historians say that France's application of Fayol's profound organizational teachings was what permitted the country to maintain civil and economic stability between the Franco-Prussian War and the First World War. By utilizing his identified functions of management, the French government was able to recover from a disastrous war and achieve stability. He was, and still is, considered the "father of planning."

Fayol outlined the five primary and necessary functions of management as follows:

1. Planning: identifying work to be done and means to do it
2. Organizing: defining and synchronizing tasks
3. Staffing: selecting and training necessary numbers of workers
4. Directing: delegating instructions and orders to follow them
5. Controlling: assuring that activities conform to plans

These functions have been called the essence of management, and because of their widespread acceptance, use, and validity, these necessary functions will be examined but not in that precise order.

PLANNING

This section addresses what is believed to be the most important of Henri Fayol's identified functions of management—planning. Because many authorities' recommendations on plan construction concern the employee's involvement and contribution to the plan's success, a discussion of employee evaluations is included in this section.

Most likely and hopefully, your department has an overall plan for both day-to-day and future operations and goals for the agency. If one doesn't exist, you can greatly expand your value to the organization by developing a plan for your unit or operation that supports and adds to the goals of the agency.

This can be as simple as figuring out "What should I or what do I have to do today?" We all do this if for nothing more than to figure out what to wear or develop a schedule to avoid conflicts in upcoming activities. Sometimes we make lists or jot down items on our calendars. We do this because we don't have complete trust in our memory or maybe have just too much to remember.

This is planning in its simplest form, and for the most part, these self-systems work over short periods and for mainly insignificant items. Even so, to accomplish even the simplest of tasks, some planning is necessary.

Lewis Carroll knew this:

> **ONCE UPON A TIME,**
> Alice while walking in Wonderland encounters the Cheshire cat and asks, "Would you tell me please, which way I ought to go from here?"
>
> "That depends a good deal on where you want to get to," said the cat. "I don't much care where," said Alice. "Then it doesn't matter which way you go," said the Cheshire cat.

Simply said, you probably won't get there if you don't know where you are going. Neither will your agency. That's why you must have a plan.

A similar illustration of the necessity and importance of planning is one we take for granted each time we travel. If you wanted to sail or fly to the Orient, you wouldn't just hop on a plane or boat and set out across the Pacific. You would get a compass and a map and chart a course. You would estimate what supplies were needed—fuel, food, and so on. Throughout the trip you would check to see if you were still on course. You would then arrive at your desired destination.

More formally, planning is a fundamental management function that involves deciding what it is that needs to be done, how and when it is to be done, and who is going to do it.

Again, in your current position and level in the organization, plans you develop and implement should concern your unit and support the agency's overall plan and mission.

According to Fayol, planning is the most crucial of all the five functions of management. It is the first stage of the managerial functions. If there is no planning, there is nothing to organize, direct, or control. Planning must be continuous and never ending.

Planning requires collecting and analyzing information, determining courses of action, and selecting the best course to take. It prevents hasty decisions and, by specifying a definite course of action, aids in improving the motivation and morale of employees. Everyone likes to know where they are going.

Henri Fayol later expanded this theory to include long-range planning stretching out five or more years. This system involved obtaining future forecasts from persons both inside and outside the organization. At the time this was a radical departure from what most businesses were doing. But as the Industrial Revolution took place, detailed futuristic planning became a widely accepted practice. It was adopted by General Motors in 1930, and many believe it to be the reason that the company became a leader in the auto industry.

The importance of planning as presented by Fayol is still recognized today by contemporary management authorities. For instance, the "management by objectives" (MBO) guru **Peter F. Drucker** declared "planning to be the foundation of running an organization."

Planning via the MBO process is exactly that. It is a planning process where you figure out where you want to go, or do, or be, and make a plan to get there.

A leading proponent of the management-by-objectives concept was **George S. Odiorne**, an American academic of the last century and a student of Peter Drucker.

In his approach, Odiorne wanted the development of goals and their methods of accomplishment to be a shared process, where the superior and the subordinates jointly take part in the goal setting. Then together they identify the courses of action to be followed to achieve them.

Next, the employees were given individual performance standards designed to achieve particular objectives that contribute to goal achievement. Odiorne's rationale was that if the employees were involved in developing the goals and were assigned individual responsibilities, they would take a more personal interest in achieving them.

SOMEONE ONCE SAID:

**The more we can encourage participation,
I think the better off we are.**
—Barack Obama

Thus, another management approach, "participative management," which will be outlined later, is included in the goals-and-
objectives-setting process.

This system has the advantage of not only moving the organization toward identified objectives but provides the opportunity to
evaluate the contribution of the employees.

Odiorne listed five steps to implement his version of MBO:

1. Review organizational goals.
   Somewhere there is documented the overall purpose and reason for your agency's being. To simplify, let's assume that it
   is to "Protect Life and Property." The objectives you identify
   should contribute to this overall purpose.

2. Set worker objectives.
   Odiorne recommended involving workers in the goal setting
   where an agreed-upon level of activity or contribution by
   employees is established.

3. Monitor progress.
   As the period of the established goals progresses, measure-
   ments of progress should be made. If progress is not being
   made as scheduled, changes in the operation are called for.

4. Evaluate the process.
   At the end of the established goal period, an evaluation of
   the process should be made. Determine: Were the objectives
   achieved? What contributed to meeting the goals or prevented
   their accomplishment?

5. Reward.

If the desired result was achieved, those individuals meeting or exceeding their individual contribution goals should be rewarded.

Odiorne suggested utilizing the employees' contributions toward meeting the agency's overall goals by tying the employees' goals to those of the agency.

For example, individuals can contribute to an agency-established goal to reduce various types of crime. If the department's goal is to reduce commercial burglaries, individuals can be given an agreed-upon number of business establishments to perform security checks on during a shift. These checks often deter burglars, and while conducting one, the officer may encounter a crime in progress and make an arrest. Both of which contribute to the overall goal of reducing commercial burglaries.

Management by objectives is an accepted management tool that has been adopted by business and governments worldwide. Hewlett-Packard, Xerox, DuPont, Intel, and others all use MBO and praise its effectiveness.

Quite simply, when inserted into the managing of a unit or organization, the process of setting goals or objectives by identifying desired results, figuring out how to accomplish them, and then assigning responsibilities for that accomplishment is MBO.

During this process you must take into account necessary resources, outside influences, and perhaps obstacles.

In his book *The Peter Prescription,* **Dr. Laurence J. Peter** advised in Prescription #31, "Peter Practicality," that the goals you set must be reasonably obtainable. Do not confuse "possible" with "reasonable," he urged. If a goal is clearly unreachable, and it is recognized as such, little effort will be made to achieve it. Conversely, if a goal appears achievable, people will strive to attain it.

Many organizations, however, concentrate on the results alone and spend little time working on the method of or likelihood of achieving them.

SOMEONE ONCE SAID:

**People aren't really interested in processes
and problems, only in results. They don't
want to hear about the labor pains, they only
want to see the baby.**
—Anonymous

Some administrators simply say they are going to reduce the number of homicides in this jurisdiction, and their only plan is to try to obtain additional resources. Then only a sketchy plan is included in the budget request. This misses the purpose of MBO and often fails.

Professional management is beyond that. Even should that be the approach taken by your agency, you as a middle manager can develop more comprehensive plans for your level of operation.

Remember, however, that although goals and their achieving them are of great importance, actions taken in reaching them should not override good management practices.

ONCE UPON A TIME,
in a fairly large city, the chief of police became concerned because fatal accidents where speed was the primary cause rose more than 15 percent over a two-year period. It was noted that during the same period, the number of speed citations issued had decreased by 22 percent.

As a result, one of the goals set for the following year was to hold speed-related traffic fatalities at the same level. One of the means listed to accomplish this goal was to have the traffic division emphasize speed enforcement. This responsibility fell mainly on the motor squad. It was determined that the number of speed citations issued should be increased by 25 percent to more than offset the previous reduction.

The 4:00 p.m. to midnight shift was the largest and most active motorcycle unit, and although the term "quota" was not used, a numerical "goal" of the number of speed citations to be issued per hour was set, and if this goal was met, the annual goal would be achieved.

SOMEONE ONCE SAID:

When it is obvious that the goals cannot be reached, adjust the action steps.
—Confucius

But be careful when you do.

At midyear, the lieutenant supervising the motorcycle unit noted that the citation goal would not be met at the present rate of issuance. Speed-related accidents were staying at approximately the same level also. Something had to be done.

Because the city was considered to be a "rough" one, for officer safety reasons, departmental policy required that officers in cars double up at darkness and that motorcycle officers ride in pairs.

The lieutenant noted that once the motors paired up, their activity was cut in half. So, in order to have a chance of meeting the citation goal, it was decided that the motorcycle officers would not double up. This worked well, and it appeared that the citation goal would be met or even be exceeded.

SOMEONE ONCE SAID:

All good things must come to an end.
—Geoffrey Chaucer

It worked well until one night at the shift's end, one of the motor officers was missing. Efforts to raise her on the radio failed. The supervisors sent the entire squad back out to canvass the entire area where her beat was located. To no avail. Several additional officers in the district were called in to take part in the search. The media sought the public's assistance.

> Once it was daylight, the officer was located. While attempting to apprehend a "failure to yield," and before she could call it in, she had missed a turn, run off the road, and gone down an embankment. She was seriously injured. The non-doubling practice was curtailed, and the lieutenant disciplined.

Although goals are important, they are not *most* important!

The MBO approach to planning can be utilized at every level of the organization or even by you personally to plan your own future. As was said, it is a process of figuring out where you want to go and planning how to get there.

Remember, goals and objectives included in plans should be measurable as well as reasonably obtainable.

SOMEONE ONCE SAID:

Make time for planning:
wars are won in the general's tent.
—Stephen R. Covey

Plans for almost any endeavor are important, and their completeness and formality should correspond to their reason and intended result.

Most short-term plans needn't be written down unless it is necessary for a particularly important function and approval of your strategy from above is required. Additionally, plans that involve other agencies need to be coordinated with them.

In some cases, however, even hourly plans or specific incident plans might be necessary. Suppose, for example, that you are placed in charge of motorcading the president of the United States through your jurisdiction. Working with the Secret Service, you must have a route planned. Possible traffic congestion and the need for roadblocks must be considered. The length of the route, the time to travel it, and the number of personnel needed to control traffic must be also be included. Even though a singular occurrence of short duration, the event is important, and the plan must be comprehensive and complete.

In his book, *Police Administration*, **O. W. Wilson**, advised that there are several different types of plans and sub-plans that may be desired.

Most important is the general plan for the agency, which has been discussed. That is a management plan that outlines the department's purpose and mission and identifies goals and objectives, including the means of accomplishing them.

Wilson goes on to list financial plans, human resources plans, training plans, public relations plans, operating plans, emergency plans, and, finally, tactical plans.

Most of these are probably addressed at the agency level, but tactical plans normally apply at the street or unit level, so their necessity will be looked at.

This type of plan is more basic and localized in nature and deals primarily with initial response to incidents where necessary and immediate actions that must be taken. These plans need not be extensive, but they should be designed to offer guidance and direction when nonroutine incidents occur.

SOMEONE ONCE SAID:

Hope for the best, plan for the worst.
—Jack Reacher

Be sure to consider unknowns and possible obstacles while in the planning process. It is wise to allow for unexpected contingencies in your plan. Unusual weather, power outages, citizen reaction or outrage, and similar unexpected happenings are all possible elements that can influence the handling of an incident. They have been known to do so.

> ***ONCE UPON A TIME,***
> in a rural area, an uncontrolled fire consumed several houses and threatened several others requiring an evacuation of a large area.
>
> The sheriff's department was in charge of the evacuation and relocating the evacuees. This the department

did, sheltering them at the county fairgrounds. All went well until it was discovered that no plans had been made for the safety of the larger animals belonging to the people being relocated. During the evacuation process several citizens expressed some anxieties, but nothing was done to alleviate their concerns.

Once the fire was controlled and the people were allowed to return to their homes, they became furious upon discovering that many of their animals, including beloved horses, had perished in the fire. They blamed the sheriff, claiming that they assumed that he had taken care of their removal and safety. Instead of praise for having successfully ensured that the citizens were safe, he was castigated for not having a plan to safeguard their animals.

In this line of work anything can happen and often does.

The mishandling of some seemingly routine incidents can be almost as disastrous as an actual catastrophic one. The types of occurrences that do happen where most likely no type of plan exists can range from a high-profile kidnapping to the unnatural death of a newsworthy person, a multiple-fatality traffic accident, or, as noted, a fire where animals might be endangered.

SOMEONE ONCE SAID:

To expect the unexpected shows a thoroughly modern intellect.
—*Oscar Wilde*

These types of incidents may not require a total agency plan, but the division, section, unit, or whatever tasked with the responsibility to provide a response should have a basic plan prepared if and when these incidents do occur.

At a minimum, basic plans should answer the following questions:

1. What additional response might be required from your agency?
2. What allied agency assistance might be needed?
3. What resources might be needed? Aircraft, off-highway vehicles, and so on.
4. Who should be contacted? If possible, identify specific individuals.
5. Who should be notified?
6. Who will handle the media, both professional and social?
7. Who will complete the investigation? Reports? Prosecution?
8. Anything else that you can think of.

These plans should be local and specific to a geographical area, or to a unit's particular responsibilities, and must be coordinated with the department's overall emergency plan.

ORGANIZING AND UNITY OF COMMAND

The reason for organizing is elementary. Disorganization is wasteful and nonproductive. Having the correct structure of the group and identifying and assigning the specific responsibilities and functions to the various units and ranks are necessary to assure efficiency and assist in the achievement of an organization's goals. It is addressed by two means: organization of the work and organization of the people.

Every organization has or should have a chart that clearly delineates the responsibility and function of the various levels of command and the various units. These are normally pyramidal in shape, having management at the top, with supervisors and then the workers below. Staff units are shown laterally at the various levels. This is termed a scalar process, and it illustrates the vertical levels of authority and responsibility. Simply, which unit does what and who reports to whom?

SOMEONE ONCE SAID:

Diversity in counsel, unity in command.
—Cyrus the Great

In other words, it is acceptable to get and give advice from many, but only one should give the orders.

"Unity of command" as an accepted principle in organizational structure simply means that employees should have only one boss. In the chapter "Notes on the Theory of Organization" from his book *Papers on the Science of Administration*, **Luther Gulick**, when defining "organizing," made the point, "A man cannot serve two masters."

Even though there are several levels in what is termed the chain of command over an employee, the next highest level only should be his or her boss. Directives and communications must follow the chain in both directions. This is necessary to avoid conflicts and misunderstandings. Gulick emphasized that direct control over an employee should be restricted to one individual.

Historically, every authority seems to have agreed with this premise; recently, however, its value has been questioned by modern theorists who claim that this rigidity is overly bureaucratic and often slows and encumbers progress.

In *Models of Discovery*, **Herbert Simon**, another political scientist, cognitive psychologist, and author, asserted that unity of command interferes with specialization. At present numerous units in most organizations require expertise in decision making and resultant actions, and sometimes line managers do not have that expertise and cannot provide suitable direction. Thus, specialized control may be necessary outside the normal command chain.

These conditions may exist in your agency. If so, alternatives to the strict unity-of-command edict might involve delegation of certain decision-making and direction-giving functions to those individuals qualified to handle them.

Consideration should be given to formally establish separate command chains for use only in cases where particular knowledge is specific to some highly specialized units. Examples might include evidence specialists, a jail or coroner operation, or the communications unit that may need its own chain of command. Many times a line manager cannot give proper oversight to these functions and must rely on the experts who work there to oversee them.

However, deviations in the formal chain should not erode management's overall authority. Direction from the top should follow the chain of command downward, with each level in compliance, even though there may be slight divergence in specialist units.

These exceptions aside, by definition the chain of command is the official hierarchy of authority that dictates who is in charge of whom and who tells whom what to do. It is the order in which authority and power in an organization is wielded and delegated from top management to all employees.

It has long been believed that a chain of command and adherence to it are vitally necessary for an organization's successful operation. A chain of command provides the ability for management to control a great number of people and operations and prevents the chaos that would result from everyone "doing their own thing."

Even so, there are recognized disadvantages to a formal chain of command. It tends to slow communications. If working properly, the chain requires that a directive from the controlling executive be handed down from each level of command to the one below it. Thus, the more levels, the more handing down that must be done. In addition to slowing the process, it increases the opportunity for misunderstanding. The same is true for information starting at the bottom of the chain, intended for top management.

In most law enforcement agencies, the highest on the chain is the chief, the sheriff, the colonel, or the superintendent. From there the ranks normally descend to the rank of patrol officer.

And in most law enforcement agencies, the highest on the chain is there for a reason. He or she has somehow survived in the profession. In spite of the fact that some may not always live up to the highest standard, the majority have searched for and found that "excellence" described in **Tom Peter's** and **Robert Waterman's** best seller *In Search of Excellence*. They supervise, they manage, they lead, and they have survived. Thus, it follows that in most cases their directives should effortlessly roll down the chain and be respected and followed.

The purpose of your agency should dictate its organization. Even so, there can be many variables. Essentially, though, most departments are organized by function, and most likely your agency is the same. Units such as administration, patrol, investigations, communications, and so on were formed based on their purpose and role.

The "line" and "'support" units are normally compartmentalized. Geography is another form of organization. In large jurisdictions, separate geographical districts are formed, and each has its own components and command structures, with each district reporting to the central command or headquarters.

Again, the important element is that each unit, no matter how formed, should have an identified chain and be led by competent individuals.

The number of links or levels of rank in the chain are dependent on the variety of tasks to be performed and the relative difference and skill sets required to effectively perform at each level.

Size of the organization is a consideration but not necessarily the determining factor. Worldwide, the Catholic Church has approximately 408,000 employees and has basically four levels of command. The pope, cardinals, bishops, and priests guide and direct the organization. The church has been in successful operation for more than two thousand years and provides service to more than two billion people.

By contrast, most large police organizations with perhaps a thousand personnel have up to ten levels of command. There are the chief, deputy chief, assistant chiefs, chiefs of operations, division or sector chiefs, patrol chiefs, captains, lieutenants, sergeants, and corporals.

Both of these models provide for well-run, productive, and efficient organizations. The church, even though widely geographically spread, has similar functions and operations throughout the world. Conversely, the police department has diverse functions and responsibilities, many requiring specialization.

In his book *Human Behavior at Work*, **Keith Davis**, a recognized management educator, addressed the classical theory of organization that rather change the jobs to fit the people, organizations should train the people to fit the jobs. This is because it is assumed that people will come and go, but the jobs will remain fairly constant. Yet, he argued, this should not be a hard-and-fast rule. People are different and have different strengths and weaknesses. Sometimes the job can be altered to fit the individual to the advantage of the organization.

With respect to assignment of work in law enforcement agencies, the common breakdown is "line" and "staff," basically meaning operational functions and administrative roles.

However, quite often there is some overlap between the two. For example, the commander of a field operation may have assigned duties that are almost entirely administrative, yet the commander will be primarily in charge of a line function. This is a common arrangement, but it often results in problems if the individual does not allot the correct amount of interest to each function. Most often, since the career history of the individual has been the line function, it is the administrative responsibilities that suffer.

ONCE UPON A TIME,
a newly promoted captain was assigned to the position of commander of a field operations division. The captain was an immediate success. Arrests were up, and calls for service were down as were felony crimes. Under his direct supervision, a hostage situation was handled without injury to anyone. His future was looking bright.

Unfortunately, up to this point in his career, he had never really been schooled in administrative functions and responsibilities.

The department required that subordinate commands submit a quarterly report outlining activities that had occurred during the period. The report had to be detailed and on time. The department also required that an effort/expenditure-versus-results analysis be made, kind of like a cost/benefit ratio, in order to measure some programs effectiveness.

The captain's supervisor noted that these reports were not sufficiently detailed and frequently late. Further, they regularly contained errors.

When budget time rolled around, it was each commander's responsibility to submit justified requests for any increases and substantiation for the ongoing funding of any special programs. Again, the captain's supervisor was disappointed in his submission. The supervisor's initial thought was that this was a case of the renowned Peter Principle—the captain had been promoted to the level that exceeded his ability. This was, however, countered by the captain's day-to-day performance as a line commander.

Investigation disclosed that the captain had been given minimal training on the various administrative functions and had not performed most of them as a lieutenant. Those that he had experience in had been done under direct supervision. Now as a commander, he had little skill or interest in administration, just operations.

> Once brought to light, improvement was made and he retained his position, but the observed deficiencies cost the captain his next promotion.

Even if certain functions are outside your comfort zone, they must be performed if required. They might not be of real interest to you, but there is a reason for requiring and performing them. It's your place in the organization.

SOMEONE ONCE SAID:

The superior man makes the difficulty to be overcome his first interest; success only comes later.
—Confucius

Again, in some cases the operations of line and staff may overlap, but to be successful, both must be given their due. This is why attention to the "organization" of the agency is important and is included as one of Henri Fayol's top five requirements for a successful operation.

DIRECTING

Throughout the years, numerous theories of how to provide direction, more commonly known as supervision, have been studied. They vary greatly and have been discussed at length by management theorists and experts.

Douglas McGregor's Theory X and Theory Y approaches were discussed previously. They address the basic giving of orders, either in a pleasant manner or in a harsher way. To improve the chances for success, later experts recommend that Theory Y, or the polite method, be employed when directing subordinates.

Beginning in the early 1980s, two prominent and recognized management authorities, **Ken Blanchard** and **Spencer Johnson**, instructed a type of "participative directing" in their book *The One Minute Manager*.

Their concept was that several management functions could be and should be accomplished in just a few minutes.

They proposed that a manager should work with an individual employee and spend one minute setting goals, one minute praising the employee for achieving the goals, and one minute reprimanding the employee for individual faults or for not meeting the goals.

Blanchard and Johnson have recently updated the book to make the process more collaborative and to include praise in the reprimand phase, terming it "redirect." In other words, "You didn't do so well, but thank you for your efforts, and here is how you can improve."

The one-minute concept follows the general pattern of MBO except it requires the manager to meet with the employee and agree on simple goals, jotting them down in a few sentences.

These goals and progress toward them then must be frequently reviewed at one-minute meetings.

SOMEONE ONCE SAID:

What's measured improves.
—Peter F. Drucker

At these one-minute meetings, the praise and/or redirect steps are brought into play. The employee is either praised for meeting the goals or admonished for not meeting the goal but praised for trying.

The authors claim that the benefits of this approach are the employee's initial buy-in of the goals, the fairly instant rewards for success, and timely correction of mistakes. They claim that this is more effective than a once-a-year goal-setting conference and then waiting for a quarterly or annual performance appraisal to provide feedback.

This more frequent attention also gives the employee knowledge that the supervisor is interested in him or her.

Further, it could result in a positive behavior change as demonstrated in B.F. Skinner's motivation and rewards theory. Recognition results in positive action.

This simple and efficient approach provides the supervisor with a controlled and consistent method of directing and managing.

The main drawback would seem to be the difficulty a manager would have spending even just a minute with each subordinate. If the manager had many subordinates, he or she may not have time to go through the various phases of the approach so frequently. Also, it may be ineffective if the supervisor did not have a pretty intimate knowledge of each employee's skills and abilities.

SOMEONE ONCE SAID:

Set specific outcomes,
but not a detailed process.
—Marcus Buckingham

Rather than combining the providing of direction with goal setting and performance evaluation, a better approach might be to make the setting of goals for the upcoming year a part of an employee's annual evaluation and then have periodic sit-downs or meetings with the employee. At these meetings, informally review the department's or unit's current goals and objectives and discuss the individual's performance and contribution in reaching those goals.

Again, these meetings need not be formal, but they do give you the opportunity to reinforce the agency's goals and your interest in them. And by so doing, you can perhaps boost the employee's interest in them. Many times, if employees believe that you support the goals, they will too.

These meetings, if held frequently enough, shouldn't take much more than "one minute." But it is essential that you get all of the department on board for the process to be successful.

ONCE UPON A TIME,
a department had adopted Drucker's MBO procedures for goal setting, including the required the periodic meetings with subordinates to reinforce the program.

One middle manager did not really like the process, but since the department wanted it done, she would do it. In doing so, she would, in a formal memo, direct employees to meet in her office.

Once the employee was in the office, she would begin the interview by commanding "Sit down! Let's get this over with!" in a very serious and authoritarian manner (borderline Theory x).

Her subordinates interpreted this opening as a clear indication that the manager didn't want to be there, and the employees would mirror this perceived attitude. As a result, the meetings were unproductive and meaningless.

Top management noticed that the process was having problems and soon determined that it was just one particular manager who seemed to be creating them.

She was not called "on the carpet" but instead was counseled by her supervisor about the department's belief in the system, her importance in making it work, and the necessity for her to alter her approach.

As a corrective measure, several of her subsequent interviews were recorded. This led to the discovery that although she conducted the interviews competently, it was her manner in doing them that led to the less than desirable results. Whether intended, or just through habit, her commanding attitude compromised the meeting's intention of directly involving employees in the department's goal achievement process. They were so intimidated that they missed the entire point of the process.

Once the manager's obvious negative manner was brought to her attention, necessary correction was made. The formal directive memo was eliminated, and the meetings began with "Thanks for coming in. Please have a seat. The reason you're here is that we need your input."

It worked. Both the manager and her subordinates became involved in and contributed to the process.

Methods matter. Sometimes the little things make a difference.

This sit-down process, if done as intended, also gives you the opportunity to recognize your subordinates' accomplishments or provide corrective direction without waiting for a formal personnel evaluation. It also reinforces employees' belief that management cares about them.

SOMEONE ONCE SAID:

The deepest desire of the human spirit is to be acknowledged.
—Stephen R. Covey

In their book *Contact: The First Four Minutes*, psychiatrists **Leonard and Natalie Zunin** explain that there is a short period, a four-minute window of opportunity, when a satisfactory relationship can be established or rejected. Thus, is it critical that the interview get off on the right foot. The Zunins explain that if you don't make a conscious effort to make a positive impression at the beginning of the contact, you will be thought of as disinterested or uncaring for the discussion subject or the individual, or both.

You need to do these four things in the first four minutes:

1. Project confidence. Make it obvious that you know the subject to be discussed and that you are embarking on a positive discussion.
2. Use creativity. Take the time beforehand to determine a course of action and imagine the employee's probable response. Be prepared to change course if the response is quite different from what you expected.
3. Demonstrate caring. To make the interview truly successful, you must clearly demonstrate your interest to the employee. No glancing at your email or iPhone or engaging in other distracting behavior during the conversation. You must give him or her your total attention. Again it is advised that you inquire about the individual's well-being, family, or concerns without getting too personal.
4. Show consideration. Focus on what you can say, and how you say it, so at the end of the conversation, employees will leave feeling better about themselves.

SOMEONE ONCE SAID:

**Interpersonal politics,
that's what it's all about.**
—Max Cannon

So now you have a "four-minute" conference plan that also stresses that you should follow the Theory Y style to be successful.

CONTROLLING

Somewhere in your training, you probably learned that positioning was important when dealing with people. Proper positioning offered an advantage with respect to control, so you probably practiced it when dealing with the public.

Expanding on this, **Michael Connelly** reinforces the theory in his best seller *The Gods of Guilt*, although a work of fiction. He has the Lincoln Lawyer explain that a recognized method of discreetly controlling a conversation is to place the person you are conversing with to your right, even if face-to-face, so that they will be looking toward you from their left. This positioning gives you some type of psychological advantage. "It's a right brain, left brain thing." Although probably not clinically proven, it seems to work.

If it is good-enough method of control for the Lincoln Lawyer, you should possibly employ it in your personal contacts.

Frederick Winslow Taylor was a contemporary of Henri Fayol. But his approach to improving production and employee relations was almost the complete opposite of Fayol's.

Rather than placing emphasis on the five necessary functions of management, Taylor recommended a system that concentrates on the process rather than the plan. He believed that by improving the methodology by which something was done, favorable results would follow.

Taylor was an industrial engineer who at the time was recognized as the "father of scientific management." His book *The Principles of Modern Management,* written in 1911, illustrates his approach to industrialized management. This was the period when factories and their mass production methods were becoming the norm and replacing small shop operations. The automobile industry in particular adopted Taylor's teachings.

His scientific management theory, called "Taylorism," was based on his belief that in the past, people had been management's primary consideration, but in the future, the system must be first.

Taylor developed his theory by observing workers in factory production jobs. He diligently observed, recorded, and timed their actions, conducting actual time-motion studies. Through detailed study of these actions he was able to improve some procedures and eliminate others. This management method was particularly adaptable to assembly-line manufacturing.

Exact and set procedures for each function were established, and management was assigned the responsibility of ensuring that the workers abided by the approved systems and methods.

SOMEONE ONCE SAID:

It is only through enforced standardization of methods, enforced adoption of the best implements and working conditions that this faster work can be assured. And the duty of enforcing the adoption of standards rests with management alone.
—*Frederick Taylor*

Taylor's recommended method for accomplishing this "enforcement duty" was to arrange the workplace so that management could enforce the standards by directly observing the workers. Factories were built with the boss's office having windowed walls and being placed in the center of the workplace or overlooking it. As can be imagined, this approach might be very effective as far as management is concerned, but it would be very intimidating to the workers.

It was this type and style of management that brought about labor unions to defend the workers. This organizing of the workers did much to reduce Taylorism as a management control system.

Plus, now that most work is performed outside the factory, most situations do not allow for management's continual observation of employees. Voluntary compliance on the part of the worker is now the more important part of the process.

But this may be changing. Modern technology may once again permit management to observe workers' activities and distantly control them. Cameras are everywhere. Many are in positions that can observe employees at work.

Even law enforcement may not be escaping this regressive control method. With the advent and use of GPS, the constant tracking of patrol units is a reality in many police agencies. Big brother can once again monitor the workers' every move. Management must utilize this methodology sparingly.

Another approach, again almost the complete opposite of Taylor's, suggests that management's interest should be centered on the worker and working conditions, not the number or amount produced. This approach also suggests that proper investment in and development of employees would result in superior results. Quality results.

SOMEONE ONCE SAID:

**Quality management is not just a step.
It must be a new style of working.
Even a new style of thinking.
The dedication to quality and excellence
is more than good business; it's a way of life.**
—*George H. W. Bush*

Stanford University professor **W. Edwards Deming** was another widely acknowledged management thinker. He is recognized as the individual who helped Japan get back on its feet economically after the Second World War. He observed that in Japan's postwar industrial complex, the entire emphasis of management was on production and process, and little attention was paid to the conditions of workers or the guidance provided to them. Deming instituted a complete renovation of Japan's management practices and philosophies. This was done by having management concentrate on a philosophy similar to Maslow's except for "bean counting." Rather than concentrating on production, he pushed attention to the workforce and quality in the workplace. Proof of his success is that after a couple of years, about 15 percent of products purchased in the United States had a "Made in Japan" label attached.

Deming used this same approach in the 1980s in Detroit. The Ford Motor Company, concerned with falling sales, hired Deming to redefine and restructure the company's management culture. By simply altering management practices, Ford soon came out with better-quality vehicles and became the country's most profitable auto manufacturer. Again, Deming did not concern himself with the number of parts or cars an individual produced; instead he concentrated on improved working conditions and employee treatment, and the production problems improved accordingly.

Deming is known for an innovation that he termed "total quality management," which concentrates on management's positive actions rather than establishes hard-and-fast rules and production quotas for employees. To implement it, management must:

1. Create consistency of purpose.
2. Adopt and institute leadership.
3. Drive out fear.
4. Break down barriers between staff areas.
5. Institute a vigorous program of education and self-improvement for everyone.
6. Institute on-the-job training.

For the most part, Deming's principles are universally accepted as methods that management should be using to make an organization successful. Even though they were designed for and used in industry, they can be applicable in a law enforcement agency.

Again, as was noted earlier, it is management's job to create a climate where people want to succeed and where they can succeed. And that's the climate Deming's principles are designed to create.

Deming, in his book *Out of the Crisis*, which instructs on these "total quality management" principles, included some thoughts that directly contradict the philosophies of most recognized authorities:

1. Eliminate work standards (quotas). Substitute with leadership.
2. Eliminate management by objectives and management by numbers and all numerical goals. Substitute with leadership.
3. Eliminate slogans, exhortations, and targets for the workforce levels of productivity, as these create adversarial relationships. Substitute with leadership.

His belief was that numerical standards should be replaced by quality goals. By improving management practices, offering education programs, and instilling leadership whose goal is to assist the workers, management can improve both the quality and quantity of production.

Most authorities agree that good management should include interest in the employees and a good work environment, but that these must be coupled with adequate and reasonable controls. A combination of all these factors leads to success.

Critics of Deming have pointed out that a key element of control is the measurement of activity. Not just numbers, but the value of the output.

SOMEONE ONCE SAID:

It is the quality of our work which will please god and not the quantity.
—Mahatma Gandhi

Henri Fayol's approach to control was defined as "seeing that everything occurs in conformity with established rule and expressed demand."

Probably the most recognized method of obtaining conformity with the established rule and maintaining control in an organization is through the existence of policies that direct behavior.

These are the written rules, both general and specific, that outline required behavior and actions in most aspects of the organization's operations. They are necessary in securing consistency of action. For the most part, policies generally cover a broad area, and it is under them that standard operating procedures (SOPs) are developed to address specifics.

SOMEONE ONCE SAID:

Rules and responsibilities: those are the ties that bind us.
—Neil Gaiman

Unless the organization that you are moving up in or into is brand-new, it should have a policy manual. It will cover everything from instruction on the use and number of forms required to acceptable conduct and expected performance.

There is normally a requirement that every member of the department be knowledgeable of and obedient to these directives.

An organization is controlled through these rules and established procedures, and one of the primary responsibilities of supervisors and managers is to ensure compliance with them.

Law enforcement litigation expert **G. Patrick Gallagher**, in his book *Risk Management Behind the Blue Curtain,* outlined a series of steps to take with regard to directives needed to establish necessary control:

- Establish necessary policies and procedures.
- Train all individuals in them.
- Implement them in an organized fashion.
- Provide supervision to assure compliance.
- Review and revise as necessary.

Gallagher doesn't promise total immunity from harm if the recommended measures are taken, but by following them, uniformity of desired actions is enhanced and risk reduced.

Care must be taken because there are some instances where informal policy decisions replace what is actual departmental policy. This is done by officers and supervisors who sometimes bend the rules for operational ease.

For example, there may be a policy that officers cannot leave their beats to take a break. But occasionally there are no suitable establishments on their beat and a supervisor will let them go to an adjacent beat for breaks or lunch. This is in fact a policy violation, but normally a harmless one, and unless things get out of hand, it is overlooked by management.

Be aware, however, that sometimes an informal bending of the rules can have serious results.

ONCE UPON A TIME,
in a medium-size department there was a written policy that stated:

All uniformed members of the department shall receive behind-the-wheel pursuit driver training at least every 3rd year.

The state highway patrol made a two-day course in high-speed driving available to local departments. It included vehicle pursuit training.

One evening an officer got into a pursuit and as a result was involved in an accident.

Even though the officer was utilizing the emergency lights and siren as required, when he ran a stop sign, he collided with a vehicle already in the intersection and an occupant in the vehicle was killed.

The officer sustained minor injuries and the pursued vehicle escaped.

The department was sued by the family of the deceased individual, and it was determined that the officer had not attended the pursuit training as required by departmental policy in over four years.

Investigation disclosed that the lieutenant in charge of training had knowingly violated the required training policy.

Apparently, another officer in the department had been involved in two high-speed collisions within the past year, so the lieutenant had assigned that officer to the training rather than the one who should have been scheduled to attend. This resulted in the second officer being outside policy when he was involved in the fatal accident.

Although on the surface sound, this reasoning didn't hold up in court. This seemingly insignificant breach of policy cost the city a great deal.

As a twenty-first-century manager, you are expected to maintain adequate control over whatever segment of the organization you are overseeing. Although it is important that you have some flexibility in that oversight, to exercise it may involve risk.

Care must be taken when developing policies not to make them overly strict and when possible build in room for reasonable flexibility. But the reason for policies is to maintain control, and care must sometimes also be taken not to allow McGregor's participative management approach to get out of hand either.

ONCE UPON A TIME,
a graveyard-shift sergeant became fed up with the amount of repetitious crime that occurred each night and his troops' seeming inability to do anything about it.

The normal deployment plan was to cover the district and assign each officer a beat, for which the officer was responsible. This geographical distribution of resources often ended up in an unequal distribution of workload. Some areas had numerous calls for service each shift, while others had relatively few. Crime was distributed similarly with both high and low areas of occurrence. Yet officers on the low-activity beats had to patrol there for coverage, unless needed for backup or an emergency in another part of the county.

Management's rationale for this was that each citizen and property owner paid for protection and that protection should be equally provided.

The sergeant was not in agreement with this policy, believing that crime prevention and apprehension of criminals were the major responsibilities of the police. In line with this belief, he pretty much abandoned the geographical deployment approach of providing coverage. Just by paying attention to what was going on, he identified the high-crime-activity areas and would on a rotational basis deploy his entire shift to that area, leaving the rest of the district pretty much uncovered. If a call came in for one of those areas, unless it was an extreme emergency, the caller would just have to wait.

As can be imagined, the change resulted in some positive results, arrests went up, and there was a noticeable positive impact on crime. The officers liked being where the action was, and once the word got out, there were numerous volunteers to work his shift, which was now unofficially called the "F**k - 'em Team."

Citizens in the neglected areas soon noticed a definite lack of service. Suspicious circumstances, prowlers, loud parties, and minor disturbances had a delayed response, if any at all. It didn't take long for management to receive complaints from the public.

Mid-management was directed to look into the situation and correct it. The sergeant and some of the team were brought in to discuss what was termed "responsibility overreach." But on reflection, it was determined that the approach taken did have some novelty and value.

The managers involved proposed an altered version of the F**k 'em Team. They discussed establishing an actual team to combat high-crime situations rather than robbing the patrol coverage. This would result in fewer personnel being assigned to a couple of patrol shifts and some beat reorganization; however, it was believed to be worth a try.

Top management approved the concept on a trial basis. The team would be led by the sergeant and would, as noted, concentrate on high-crime areas, particularly where gangs, drugs, assaults, robberies, and human trafficking were prevalent.

The name was changed to the "Find 'em Team," and after a highly successful six-month operational trial, it was made permanent.

Although the initiation of this project was clearly responsibility overreach on the sergeant's part, somewhere there was a happy medium between strict control and the use of an individual's core instinct and talent.

It should be noted that the sergeant did not need studies and statistics to identify the problem. He was aware of it just by being on the ground. The lesson here: management can benefit by keeping more informed of what's happening on the streets. This is done by establishing a close relationship with the people who are out there.

SOMEONE ONCE SAID:

It is important to remember that the word control does not mean to dominate.
—*Dr. William Glasser*

It is difficult but possible to maintain control of operations without discouraging or repressing innovation. Communicating with and listening to your subordinates are a must.

STAFFING

The importance of proper staffing was another of the basic management principles identified by Henri Fayol.

Staffing is the process of management that is concerned with obtaining, utilizing, and maintaining a satisfactory and effective workforce.

SOMEONE ONCE SAID:

Nothing we do is more important than hiring and developing people. At the end of the day you bet on people not strategies.
—Lawrence Bossidy

Although it is realized that most staffing decisions are controlled by others, staff numbers are dependent on budgets and staffing procedures are controlled by human resources units, either within or separate from your agency. Even so, proper staffing is still a major concern, for it greatly impacts the operation of the organization.

By definition, staffing is the managerial function of recruiting, selecting, training, developing, promoting, and evaluating personnel.

In their leading instructional text *Principles of Management*, fourth edition, **Harold Koontz** and **Cyril O'Donnell** devoted some sixty-three pages to staffing. They discussed in detail the purpose, process, principles, and problems of staffing. They recommended "how-tos" in the following areas:

- Correct staffing will ensure that all positions in the organization are filled by the right people who are competent and willing to discharge their responsibilities.
- Proper selection, training, compensation, and appraisal are based on the information obtained through job analysis.
- Open competition in selection and placement assures employment of the most competent and qualified staff.

Unless you are assigned to a specialized unit, most of these duties will be performed by someone else.

And although all of these functions are important, perhaps the most important is the selection and hiring of good people. If the individuals hired are reasonably intelligent, moral, and interested in a law enforcement career, their training, development, and supervision will be much easier.

SOMEONE ONCE SAID:

Hire character, train skill.
—Peter Schultz

As noted, your agency may not have a great deal of involvement in the hiring process, given civil service requirements, but it is essential that you have at least some input. Assuming that the basic requirements for employment have been established—age, height, education level, minimum examination score, etc.—there is one more important area that merits concern, but is rarely questioned. That is the individual's reason for wanting to pursue a career in law enforcement.

This is a simple question to ask, either in the formal QAP (qualifications appraisal panel) interview, or through questioning during the background investigation.

In 9 out of 10 times, the answer will be "to serve the public and make the world a safer place" or something similar. Many wish to join because a relative or hero was a cop. In most cases these are accurate responses.

Candidates are not going to articulate a desire to be given power over fellow citizens or to intimidate via being legally armed, or to express the view that being a cop gives them the means to retaliate against perceived grievances against a particular class of people. Unfortunately, whether admitted or not, these are sometimes underlying reasons for wanting to be a law enforcement officer.

SOMEONE ONCE SAID:

Instead of a man of peace and love, I have become a man of violence and revenge.
—*Hiawatha*

Again, very few individuals will disclose any prurient motive; they may not even be aware of it. But if there is a hint or suspicion of any improper desires, it should be noted and followed up on if possible.

ONCE UPON A TIME,
In a medium-size department, a young officer was hired after doing exceptionally well on both the written and oral parts of the exam. He was physically fit and displayed extreme enthusiasm.

After break-in, he consistently signed up for night shift and a beat in the "roughest" part of town. He quickly achieved one of the highest arrest stats in the department. These arrests though, were mainly for prowling or trespassing. He was known to harass loiterers and even made an arrest for the defunct law of vagrancy. As time went by, there were numerous complaints from the arrestees and occasionally from the citizens who had initially contacted the department about a problem. Several of the incidents involved an individual being taken into custody for wandering the streets late at night for no apparent reason. A mother complained that her son had been arrested for a curfew violation after she had sent him to a neighbor's on an errand.

Shortly after having spent one year on the job, the officer was involved in a shooting where he shot an unarmed peeping tom. He claimed that the suspect had made a furtive move to his waist area, and the shooting was termed justified.

The numerous arrests of citizens for seemingly just being out and about at night continued, as did the complaints. The officer's supervisors questioned and counseled him regarding these events, and he would slack off somewhat, only to resume the practice after a short interval.

Then a few months later he was involved in another shooting. This time it was fatal. Around ten o'clock one evening, the officer observed an individual standing on a ladder, apparently looking into a window at the rear of a house. As the officer confronted him, the man turned suddenly with an object in his hand and the officer shot and killed him. It turned out that it was the man's home and he had been disturbed by the rattling of a window screen, which he had been attempting to fasten. He had a hammer in his hand.

This time an in-depth investigation was conducted, including a series of interviews with a city-hired psychologist who examined the officer's past behavior and penchant for prowlers. It turned out that the officer's bride-to-be had been raped and murdered by a prowler. They had been high school sweethearts and she had waited for him to finish a military enlistment. Just prior to his return, she had been killed. He had abandoned his plan to attend college and became a police officer instead.

As a part of his analysis, the psychologist reviewed a recording of the officer's hiring interview. When asked why he wanted to join the force he had replied: "There are some really bad people out there, and I want to take care of them."

Although seemingly innocuous at the time, the statement was certainly a possible indicator of future behavior, which perhaps should have been followed up on. A required psychological exam prior to employment, if not in place, should be considered.

SOMEONE ONCE SAID:

Revenge may be wicked, but it's natural
—William Makepeace Thackeray

Again, you may have little involvement in the selection process and will most likely be concerned only with assignment, development, and oversight of those employees assigned under you.

You must, though, keep abreast of changes within the organization or in the world it serves that will affect staffing and/or training needs.

As new problems and programs emerge, operational needs will change and staffing must be altered to address them. This might include the numbers and qualifications of employees needed. You may be the one responsible for recommending and/or making the necessary changes.

SPAN OF CONTROL AND SCHEDULING

Once your agency is properly staffed and a chain of command established, the next mission is to determine what's called a "span of control." Most likely this was initially determined at the executive level. As positions and responsibilities change, so should the "span," and it will fall on you to recognize the need for change and either recommend change or make it.

Basically, span of control is an amorphous concept covering all levels of command in the organization. How many people are effectively supervising how many people doing what?

There are really no formulas that can be used to establish an optimum span of control. In many agencies, various structures are experimented with until they fail and then another is tried. As noted, the Catholic Church does very well for the most part having a huge span of control at each level.

Depending on the number of people employed and how the department is organized, the next important consideration is how many supervisors it will take to effectively supervise how many people. And how many managers can effectively manage how many supervisors. And how many managers the leaders can effectively lead.

A proper span of control is necessary because a supervisor can only be in one place at a time and cannot work twenty-four hours a day. Yet it is recognized that at least minimal supervision must be provided for most functions every day and around the clock.

The number of persons within a particular supervisor's span depends on the locations of the workers in relation to the supervisor, the complexity of the job, the subordinate's ability, and available resources.

In an organizational setting like the one recommended by Frederick Taylor, where the employees are in almost constant view of a supervisor, the span of control can be larger. In a field operation, where employees are spread over a large area, doing different tasks, the span should be smaller.

There is no set formula; however, it is recognized that the smaller the span the better.

Sometimes a department head can have a relatively small span, consisting of a single subordinate or only a couple of immediate subordinates.

This is often determined by the leader's comfort level, the capabilities of the immediate assistants, and of course the budget.

As the ranks descend, the span will by necessity increase. There will be several organizational units, most requiring individual supervision, such as patrol, investigations, communications, and clerical. Sometimes these may even be broken down further. Traffic may be separate from patrol, and investigations can be segregated by types and seriousness of crimes.

In larger departments there will be numerous administrative units such as personnel, fiscal, training, records, and so on.

A function such as patrol will require a smaller span of control because of the diverse types of functions and the distances and hours involved. Plus, supervisory assistance in decision making and problem solving is frequently required. Although there is no recognized established ratio of officer to sergeant, it is generally accepted that an officer should be able to contact a supervisor within minutes and be in physical contact with one in less than a half hour. Again, this depends the variables of numbers, jurisdiction size, and experience and abilities of the officers supervised.

In other units, the span can be much larger. In clerical or communications, for example, where the employees are centrally located and performing essentially the same tasks, most times one supervisor is all that is required for the entire unit, so the span of control for the supervisors can be much larger.

Higher up the chain, the span will narrow as organizationally the need for a high number of managers and leaders lessens. This forms the agency pyramid spoken of in the section on organizing. But here too, the variables of distance, job complexity, and subordinate ability are a consideration. For example, if your agency has an advanced information technology unit, you may need a knowledgeable individual to manage it. Her span might be only the individuals in that unit, but she would still need to be supervised, so another body would be added to someone's span of control.

SOMEONE ONCE SAID:

To survive modern times, an organization must have a structure that accepts change as its basic premise, lets tribal customs thrive, and fosters a power that is derived from respect, not rules.
—*Ricardo Semler*

As the organization changes, so do the spans of control. Management must be aware of the need for changes in employee responsibilities and be open to making them as well. Failure to do so will surely result in some superiors having too many or too few subordinates and some employees possibly being under-supervised or micromanaged.

In either case, your agency suffers, and this imbalance results in some supervisors, managers, and leaders working less and others harder.

Although not directly related, scheduling is involved in the personnel management area of concern. There is no problem with the normal nine-to-five shifts with holidays and weekends off. But once twenty-four-hour, seven-days-a-week coverage is required, different problems may emerge.

Historically, around-the-clock scheduling was done by assigning three eight-hour shifts, starting and ending so that shift changes occurred at the least busy times. Common shifts were midnight to eight, eight to four, and then four to midnight. Days off were scheduled on the same principle. On those days having the least activity or calls for service, more officers were off, and the shift was "fattest" when the need was greatest.

Perhaps observing how firefighters or ambulance personnel seemed to enjoy longer periods of off time, police unions started pushing for change. Those entities were often scheduled to work three or four twenty-four-hour shifts and then be off for about a week. This was possible because sleeping quarters were available for them at their stations.

One attempt was a change to a ten-hour shift. This permitted working four days and having three days off each week. The problem for the department was the overlap created on the workdays. Officers were now scheduled in three ten-hour shifts, totaling thirty hours per day per position. Six of these hours were overlapped. The money spent on the overlaps soon equaled the expense of hiring additional officers and was wasteful. Not many departments continued the ten-hour shift assignments.

Next to be tried and marginally still in use are the twelve-hour shift assignments. This results in a work schedule of three or four days, followed by employees getting four or five days off in a row. The employees love it. In addition to the fatigue the officers suffer during the final workdays in the stretch, this system has a major problem.

Twelve-hour shifts create part-time officers! Having so much free time offers the opportunity to pursue other careers. One sheriff complained that his most industrious deputies were now expending most of their energy on their own businesses. One owned a lawn service. Another, formerly a real crime fighter, now requested day shift with weekends off so she could run her disk jockey partnership. One became an Uber driver, while others went into full-time teaching. This type of schedule also allows employees to live out of the area and commute in on work days, thus reducing what is considered a vital attachment to the community they are serving.

In this world of change, this is one you may want to resist. The old five to eights aren't so bad.

If the organization doesn't seem to be running smoothly or there are problems that are hard to identify, look at your span of control.

PERFORMANCE MANAGEMENT

One of the more complex and in-depth systems in use for providing employee direction and correction is to link them to a formal evaluation program.

Elaine D. Pulakos, a recognized expert and researcher in industrial and organizational psychology, has created a system that she terms "performance management." This method of employee development centers on evaluations and appraisals. It can be used to support special assignments, transfers, and promotional decisions.

This system goes far beyond the evaluation systems being used in most police agencies. It includes a complex process containing defined roles and timelines for both management and employees.

Performance management initially requires that the organization's strategy and agency goals be developed and in place. Once the overall goals are formalized, five identified phases follow in the performance management method.

1. Performance planning. During this phase, the employee is advised of the agency's or unit's goals and what management's expectations are. Included is a discussion of the expected behavior and performance relative to supporting and contributing to these goals.
2. Ongoing feedback. This is to be a two-way process and one conducted almost daily. Frequent recognition and rewards for accomplishments must be provided, as should corrective measures when required.
3. Employee input. Employees do not actually rate themselves, but at the conclusion of the rating period, they list

their accomplishments and describe how they achieved the results they did and the impact and value of their work to the organization. This step serves to tie their efforts to the department's goals.

4. Performance evaluation. It is suggested that organizations have specific evaluation measures for the various ranks within the agency, that is, entry level, experienced, and supervisory. Ratings should include the following grading levels: below expectation, meets expectation, and exceeds expectation. Each rank must have clearly defined performance standards, so that evaluators will be consistent in their ratings.

5. Performance review. This is conducted at the end of the rating period, and assuming that the periodic feedback, as noted above, has been accomplished, it is simply a review and recap of performance during that period. Developmental/improvement plans for the employee if desired or necessary can be made at this time.

Ms. Pulakos's proposal is certainly a highly complex evaluation system. But according to her, if utilized correctly and consistently, it promises not only improved employee performance but a positive and systematic effort toward achieving the organization's purpose and goals. Pulakos's system also provides a negative process. If it documents that an employee's performance is declining, proof for the necessity and implementation of corrective action exists.

A caution, however: don't let this or a similar system rule the agency. It sometimes happens that so much importance and dedication of resources are placed on the correct implementation and administration of the processes that they become more important than the organization's actual operation, purpose, and goals.

There is certainly a vast difference between Pulakos's "performance" approach to evaluation and Blanchard and Johnson's one-minute concept or the Zunins' four-minute method. However, because of its complexity, the performance management method, in addition to employee evaluation, includes a means of measuring both the employee's efforts and progress toward the agency's goals.

Most organizations pick a system somewhere in between the accelerated and the overly comprehensive approaches.

Whichever system is used, the supervisors using it must be well trained in its application and purpose. And it must present an honest description of the performance it is evaluating. To do less is to discredit and devalue the entire effort, resulting only in a tremendous waste of time and employee resentment.

SOMEONE ONCE SAID:

The basic problem is that performance appraisals often don't accurately assess performance.
—W. Edwards Deming

Even though the practice is often thought of as cumbersome, unpopular, and generally unwanted by both the preparers and the receivers of the product, authorities do agree that a periodic employee evaluation is necessary and that it should contain the elements of reward and recognition and, if needed, behavioral documentation and improvement plans.

NO ONE EVER SAID:

Wow! I'm so excited about my performance appraisal today.
—Author

INVOLVEMENT AND ENGAGEMENT

SOMEONE ONCE SAID:

The greatest compliment that was ever paid me was when one asked me what I thought, and attended to my answer.
—Henry David Thoreau

Recently, much has been said and written about employee involvement in the management process and management's increased involvement with the workers. It is termed "engagement."

Involvement and engagement is a two-way street. Just as it is beneficial for management to allow and encourage participation by subordinates in the planning and achieving of goals, it is just as important for management to be involved in and aware of the everyday work problems and concerns of the employees. Essentially, there should be more feedback and more frequent communication up and down the chain.

The previous example of the Find 'em Team illustrated the value of communication between management levels. As noted, the sergeant did not have to rely on studies and statistical analysis to know what and where the problem was. The initial failure was that management did not know what the sergeant knew.

Employee engagement is a modernized version of McClelland's achievement and affiliation theory. Again reinforcing belief in an employee's needs for accomplishment and power. It also includes the Hawthorne effect, where it was shown that by simply paying attention to the workers, production improves.

McClelland instructs that now, however, instead of just creating the climate for the employee's satisfaction, management must be actively engaged in giving the employee the opportunity to provide input and take part in planning. This is an actual implementation of McGregor's Theory Y, participative management.

Sometimes, just listening to the troops' observations, be they complaints or recommendations, can assist in problem solving and improvements being made.

ONCE UPON A TIME,
a traffic commander in a mid-size department overheard several of the officers discussing, somewhat negatively, the huge involvement of Hispanics in traffic incidents. "If they would stay off the road, about half of our DUI problems and most of our accidents wouldn't happen" seemed to be the consensus.

The commander, realizing that there was a large concentration of Hispanics within the district, decided to verify the claim. In checking the statistics re accidents, citations, and arrests among the Hispanic driving population, the commander found that Hispanics were greatly overrepresented in traffic incidents when compared with their percentage of the population.

The commander next held an informal meeting with the officers in an attempt to better ID the problem and look for possible solutions. Two consistent problems were identified.

The first problem was that because many of the Hispanics were immigrants or first-generation citizens, some spoke little or no English. This created the second problem. They were mostly unlicensed and had little understanding of or simply did not know traffic laws.

The next step was to try to come up with a solution. Certainly, they could not teach the drivers English, but perhaps they could teach the drivers the law.

Many politicians and police administrators are reluctant to admit it, but a barrier exists between the police and the public. In most cases, it is initially just a slight distrust, which results in some hesitance for familiarity. Normally, this is overcome when public discussion is initiated with some groups or even a formal program such as Community Policing. However, when the police and the public speak different languages, the removal of this barrier is far more difficult and often impossible to remove.

The group determined that an information program, rather than just the enforcement program, which so far hadn't worked, was in order. The group also determined that the program must be conducted in Spanish and by an officer who is not readily identified as a policeman.

A sharp-appearing bilingual officer was selected and sent to public affairs training. Extensive traffic safety literature was produced in the Spanish language.

A Spanish-only public safety, borderline propaganda program was developed announcing the coming of a traffic safety savior– "a protector."

The officer was dressed as a superhero, given a sleek vehicle and name, and turned loose on the Hispanic community. His job was to educate community members in the law and help them get properly licensed. There were few formal meetings. He joined them in the fields and attended their gatherings. A series of short videos featuring him instructing traffic safety laws was produced and run on Spanish TV.

The results were outstanding! Not only were the Hispanic traffic accident involvement statistics turned around, but the agency's positive community relations with Hispanics soared. This program did for the department what *Adam-12* did for the LAPD and *CHiPs* did for the California Highway Patrol.

Although not an intended consequence, the involved officers were also positively affected. Morale improved dramatically as they took pride in their contribution and "engagement" with management in the planning, execution, and success of their plan.

The program gained such acclaim that it soon spread statewide and even went national. It was implemented in jurisdictions experiencing similar problems.

SOMEONE ONCE SAID:

Research indicates that workers have three prime needs: Interesting work, recognition for doing a good job, and being let in on things that are going on in the organization.
—Zig Ziglar

Employee engagement is valuable in that it fosters communication, positively affects behavior, and contributes to the organization's mission.

It has been said before, but it is important, so it is repeated: You must invest time and interest in employees. You must recognize achievement, listen, and provide feedback. They will benefit from your expertise and interest, and you may be exposed to new and beneficial ideas.

There's a world of difference between insisting on someone's doing something and establishing an atmosphere in which that person can grow into wanting to do it.
—Mr. Rogers

Create that atmosphere!

SETTING AN EXAMPLE

Discussed earlier was the importance of being a positive role model, and as you advance this importance increases. During your climb through the ranks, people have observed you and your actions, both from above and below. Their judgments have been critical, and a constant evaluation has been made about what kind of a person they think you are. Your attitudes, interests, and abilities have been informally examined and graded. Whether valid or not, judgments have been made.

It goes without saying that you must, by your actions, attempt to project a good image. The best possible image!

This of course means knowing your job, obeying the rules, treating people right, and, by so doing, setting a good example. It is also important that you develop good work habits.

Now that you are a mid-level manager, you must act like one. Your position and responsibilities are different. As noted previously, you are now another step more removed from doing the things that brought you into this profession. You may not like it, but probably for the most part, your job is administrative.

You are no longer normally required to work a beat, answer calls, take reports, or complete investigations. You will make very few arrests. At the management level it is technically not even your job to directly supervise those who do. These activities that you have performed or supervised are hard to give up. But you must give them up.

SOMEONE ONCE SAID:

It is our responsibilities, not ourselves that we should take seriously
—Peter Ustinov

Simply stated, try to "act your rank."

> ***Once upon a time,***
> while driving to work, the head of a smaller agency heard an emergency call come over the radio. At the same time she observed the responsible beat unit heading toward the scene but not making a Code 3 response. This seemed puzzling, so she later made an inquiry of the shift sergeant about why the officer was responding to an emergency call in a nonemergency manner. The sergeant promised to look into it. A couple of days later, the sergeant got back to her.
>
> It seems that a newly promoted lieutenant was also assigned to the shift, and the officers knew that if he was out and about and on the air, he would respond to most calls and initiate whatever action was necessary. This had earned him the nickname "Responder Rabbit."
>
> The officers knew that they could delay their response, because by so doing their workload was lessened. Normally by the time they arrived, the scene was

managed, and the lieutenant would have completed whatever initial action was required. The word was that he had even responded to and handled barking dog calls. The officers were perfectly content with the situation. The chief was not.

She called the lieutenant in and inquired about what was going on. He explained that he was only trying to help, the shift was his responsibility, and he was making sure that things were being done efficiently and correctly.

The chief then explained that yes, it was management's responsibility to make sure that things were being done right, but that he should not be doing them.

Even though he quit the practice, it took the lieutenant a great deal of time to regain the respect of the officers, overcome the poor example he had set, and live down his Responder Rabbit label.

So if you are to lead by example, you must set a good example.

Kevin Eikenberry, in his *Leadership & Learning* tutorial, lists several qualities that leaders should display.

Paraphrased below are those he considers most important:

1. Attitude. As a leader, people are watching you and observing your reactions to incidents and events. They will perhaps unconsciously model what they see. It follows then that you must present an upbeat and optimistic attitude even though the situation may not be completely positive.

2. Learning. Continuing to learn is important. If your subordinates observe you doing so, they will also continue to develop and grow. If they see that you are uninterested in progressing, or keeping on top of things, they will copy that attitude.

3. Trust. This is a two-way street. In order for your subordinates to develop trust in you, you must first trust them. You can accomplish this by not continually questioning their behavior. Unless their actions are completely out of the question, they should be accepted at face value. In return, your subordinates will not continually question your actions.

4. Setting an example means looking good and doing good. You should attempt to do the correct or close to correct thing in every situation. Remember, they are watching and, as Eikenberry stated, maybe copying you.

SOMEONE ONCE SAID:

Example is not the main thing in influencing others, it is the only thing.
—Albert Schweitzer

MANAGE BY WALKING AROUND

If you are a shift or unit commander, it is your responsibility to make sure that things are being done correctly. In a field operation, you will most likely have sergeants assigned, but that doesn't mean that you shouldn't respond to crime scenes or important incidents.

It is important for you to show up at major felonies, homicides, and so on, but not to every trespass or petty theft, lest you get labeled a "responder rabbit."

And when you do go, your function is to see if the incident is being handled correctly, not take over. If it isn't, then you can make corrections or offer corrective suggestions. Your being on scene will enable you to determine whether additional training, equipment, or additional personnel is required. Again, unless absolutely necessary, do not take over command of the situation. Offer your assistance and observe.

SOMEONE ONCE SAID:

Manage by walking around.
—Tom Peters

Even if you are primarily assigned as an administrator, you should still make it a practice to get out in the field and see what's happening. Do it on a nonroutine basis. Consider ride-alongs with the supervisors.

The same **Tom Peters**, whose thoughts we examined in his *In Search of Excellence* book, supports the getting-out-and-about concept in another of his books, *Thriving on Chaos*. In it, he says that getting out and actually observing what is going on is a necessary and positive activity for proper management. Doing so provides the ability to gather actual facts instead of the often distorted information that is passed up through the chain.

Peters advises that sometimes as you sit at your desk, what you are told may not be totally accurate. Although it may not be intentionally erroneous, it is simply shaded to make the teller not look too bad if the information contains something unpleasant. No one likes to be the bearer of bad news. Also, occasionally the teller's description of an incident may contain exaggeration as a way of gaining favor with the supervisor. Hard to believe, huh?

The real danger is that you may be making decisions on incomplete or inaccurate facts. By getting out to where the action is, you will certainly have a better idea of what is happening. And once it becomes known that you may show up at incidents, if they weren't being handled according to the book, they may start to be, and if it's known that you have firsthand knowledge of what did happen, reports may improve, accuracy-wise.

SOMEONE ONCE SAID:

**A desk is a dangerous place
from which to view the world.**
—John le Carré

DISCIPLINE

In the role of a middle manager, one of your primary responsibilities will be deciding on and administering discipline. In most cases, a problem that requires changing the behavior of an employee will come to you from the first-level supervisor with a recommendation for discipline or other corrective action. In some cases, you will be the final level of approval; in others, you will make a recommendation and forward the package on up the chain.

Although most law enforcement agencies go to great lengths to obtain fine sterling examples of humanity with which to fill their ranks, on occasion one of your charges may step slightly out of line or even go off the deep end with regard to rules, regulations, or even laws.

One of the truisms of law enforcement with regard to control is "Once they drive out the gate, they are pretty much on their own." This affords a freedom from direct supervision that is almost the complete opposite of the continual oversight and control that Frederick Taylor advocated.

Given this freedom, the opportunity for employees to engage in minor infractions is certainly present. Wandering off the beat, conducting personal business, and chatting up over friendly servers are frequent infractions. Even now with GPS tracking systems, the temptation and the opportunity to stray exist. Regrettably, there are the few who will take advantage of this lack of constant supervision. This is where discipline enters the picture.

Nothing can be more hurtful to the service than the neglect of discipline.
—*General George Washington*

Discipline is necessary in every organization, but because of the tremendous amount of discretion given to law enforcement officers in restricting a citizen's freedom, even up to taking a citizen's life, consistent and meaningful disciplinary procedures are an absolute in a law enforcement agency.

And based on law enforcement's having these extraordinary powers, the public can rightfully expect that they be wielded by conscientious and disciplined officers. And it is up to the police agency to establish and maintain an image that reflects the fulfillment of these expectations. Not only an image but an actual operation that reflects it.

Because of the vast amount of freedom from constant supervision they enjoy, some officers may take advantage of it and see themselves as being above the law and view obedience to minor rules a nuisance. Others may disregard authority regularly and intentionally.

If this should occur, and management becomes aware of it, no matter the level of misconduct or intent, it is your responsibility to initiate an investigation leading to disciplinary action if wrongdoing is discovered.

The citizens demand and deserve that law enforcement's behavior be above reproach.

Discipline is the bridge between goals and achievement.
—*Jim Rohn*

Unfortunately, the word "discipline" has attached to it an extremely negative connotation that makes it synonymous with punishment. In everyday use, however, discipline should mean "exerting control to achieve desired action."

In the majority of cases, what you want is to improve behavior and prevent recurrence of undesirable acts, not seek vengeance. Unfortunately, in some cases, though, the behavior has to result in severe administrative or even criminal punishment.

In his book *Supervising Police Personnel: Strengths-Based Leadership*, **Paul Whisenand**, a criminal justice associate professor at California State University, Long Beach, advises that "the purpose of discipline is to obtain compliance with established rules of conduct." He recommends several steps to discipline:

1. It should be immediate. Try to initiate the investigation and conclusion of the process as quickly as possible.
2. There must be a clear policy relating to behavior or misbehavior. And it should be understood by all.
3. It must be consistently applied to all employees, no favorites or villains.
4. It must be impersonal; punish the act, not the individual.
5. There should be an interactive discussion. Give the employee a chance to explain his behavior.
6. It should be a learning experience. Hopefully, the experience will teach the employee and others to not repeat the act.

These steps are paraphrased, but they do briefly outline the basic "hows and whys" and correct methods of carrying out simple discipline.

Upon the initial discovery of an alleged wrongdoing, the normal course of action, as in any investigation, is to try to gather the available facts. You interview witnesses, complainants, and the involved individuals to get their side of the story.

Most likely the first-line supervisor has done this when dealing with officers. If the transgression is serious, you, along with the supervisor, should interview the officer. This serves to impress the individual with the significance of the situation and will also give you firsthand knowledge of it.

Earlier it was noted, when dealing with a public wrongdoer, it is more effective to condemn the offense rather than the offender. This approach will assist in obtaining increased cooperation with officers as well.

The interview should be preceded by a review of the individual's background and work history. This review provides you with additional information and a better idea of whether or not the actions were on purpose, accidental, or repetitious.

If at all possible, from management's perspective, the initial steps of the investigation and interview should be conducted as informally as possible. The reason is that once the point is reached where possible disciplinary action might result, the employee is entitled to representation by the union, employee organization, or even an attorney. Once these folks are involved, progress is bound to be slowed.

DISCIPLINARY PHILOSOPHIES

SOMEONE ONCE SAID:

**There is only one sort of discipline,
perfect discipline.**
—General George S. Patton

Notwithstanding the general's opinion, there are numerous thoughts on how to approach and administer discipline. These variances are created by the several types of events that may call for discipline, their relative seriousness, the intention of the perpetrator, and the result of the act or omission. First-time and repeat offenders are of course treated differently.

Similar to that in a criminal investigation, the purpose in an administrative inquiry is to determine who, what, where, and why. The first three normally accompany the initiation of the probe. An incident, possibly outside policy or law and committed by a department member, is brought to management's attention. Once it established that an incident occurred and that the individual under suspicion may have some involvement, an investigation should be initiated. Next the "why" should perhaps be examined.

SOMEONE ONCE SAID:

**Managers owe it to the organization and
to their fellow workers not to tolerate
nonperforming individuals in important jobs.**
—Peter F. Drucker

Authorities differ on the importance of discovering the reasons behind the alleged act or omission.

In his top-selling book *Staff One: A Perspective on Police Management*, **Edward M. Davis**, former chief of the Los Angeles Police Department, took a serious and authoritarian approach to employee discipline. He believed that in police work, rules are rules, and the law is the law, and there should be no excuse for disobedience. He urged that repeat offenders be subjected to substantially increased penalties and that punishments be strict and equivalent to the seriousness of the offense. Punishment of wrongdoers sets an example and discourages others from similar behavior.

Chief Davis went on to comment that not all people deserve to be part of the law enforcement profession, only the best. Even some currently on the job are basically deficient and should not have been hired, but they somehow made it through the selection process. Others, even though initially qualified, have performed poorly or committed acts since being employed and no longer deserve to belong to a police agency. Further, it is the job of management to identify both the non-deserving and the poor performers and weed them out.

This disciplinary philosophy is termed "boundary discipline" as it establishes clear limits or boundaries on what is acceptable and unacceptable behavior and makes plain that unacceptable acts will be harshly dealt with. Pretty much a "zero tolerance" policy. This philosophy instills the belief that a transgression, no matter how slight, may be career ending. It is not known if this approach is successful or stifling. Although it encourages strict compliance with the rules, it may discourage innovative and adventurous behavior that might be beneficial.

Another philosophy taught in administering discipline to keep the troops on the straight and narrow is termed the "reality approach."

Developed by **Dr. William Glasser**, this corrective method focuses on what was done rather than the reason for doing it. He advised concentrating solely on the violation and not worrying about cause or why it was committed.

Although it is accepted that management should always take a genuine interest in its subordinates and their problems, Glasser's view was that management should avoid becoming entangled and bogged down in minor infractions. He thought that the major reason for this entanglement is searching for the causes of behavior. He explained why this is not always necessary in his book *Reality Therapy in Action*.

Glasser's reality approach means simply confronting the wrong-doer and addressing only the alleged violation. You advise the individual of the violation as you see it, and you only discuss whether or not it occurred. You do not address the cause, only the question of whether or not it occurred and if he or she is the culprit.

Once the guilt has been established, you next objectively address the situation, stating "This is what you have done, it is wrong and not acceptable, and this will be the result." End of story.

Glasser advised that not discussing the cause of the violation and why it happened eliminates excuse making, blame placing, and unnecessary argument.

Once it is established that a violation occurred and that the employee committed it, constructive steps can then be taken to move the person into more acceptable behavior.

This reality approach to discipline can work well with minor, often occurring infractions, such as occasional tardiness, straying off the assigned beat, submitting reports late, and so on. Making it even more efficient is that quite often a standard penalty can be worked out between the department and the union for each type of offense.

Employee associations and unions prefer this approach, because they don't have to worry about fighting the penalty, only the determination of the employee's guilt or innocence. Through our handling of criminal investigations we have been programmed to search for means, motive, and opportunity. Utilizing this method we can skip motive.

Again, the principle is that what happened, has happened, and in most cases, the cause is irrelevant so why argue over it. Management will apply the required discipline, and the employee will accept it. Move on.

This method, while providing documentation and some retribution, is certainly a time saver for all involved. But it does have some drawbacks.

Unfortunately, life isn't always that simple, and sometimes there are good reasons for rule violations. A simple example: An employee is late for work because of a wreck on the freeway that stalled all traffic. The tardiness violation exists, but a valid reason also exists. Further, a second employee is also late because he or she did not leave the golf course in time to go home and change clothes before reporting to work.

The reality approach would have both employees subjected to the same corrective action. Would that be fair?

The reality approach also establishes precedence and ties management's hands somewhat by predetermining a particular punishment for a particular offense. This isn't always appropriate. Repeat offenders and those who intentionally violate the rules should be treated differently than first timers and those who innocently stray.

Establishing the cause is important because accidental acts and intentional acts should be handled differently. Not knowing that the act or omission was wrong is certainly different from knowing it was wrong but doing it anyway.

Quite often the actual causes for actions cannot be established, for as you well know, people quite often do not tell the truth. With regard to policy violations, you have no doubt heard, "Gee, when did they change that?"

Punishment can be standardized for lesser offenses, but in each case, the circumstances of the specific event and the individual involved should be considered. And the gravity of wrongdoing should be stressed. If particular actions always result in similar consequences and do become routine, the importance of obedience becomes clouded and routine also.

If the violation is more serious, the reality approach should not be used as many of those cases may end up in disciplinary hearings or court, where the hearing officers or judges should not be bound by departmental policy agreements with respect to punishment.

No matter which approach is used, one problem you as a mid-level manager may encounter with discipline, is that most often the rule violations are committed by an employee not directly working for you. Perhaps the employee is a couple of steps down the chain. And unless the violation is serious, you must work through the intervening ranks to get it corrected rather than take direct action yourself. In most cases, action must be initiated and done by someone else.

To illustrate, perhaps you notice an officer who continually shows up for work in an unacceptable uniform. It is not really your job to take corrective action, but action must be taken, and the problem must be corrected.

Rather than taking on the immediate supervisor for his failure to make the correction, you might suggest that he take a look at the officer's uniform and then wait to see what happens. Maybe the supervisor didn't notice the infraction.

Handling it in this manner also gives you the opportunity to observe his problem-solving abilities. And it makes him aware of your concerns.

You can see if the problem is solved, how he went about it, and whether he was successful in that the infraction was not repeated. In either case, this may offer you an instructional opportunity.

SOMEONE ONCE SAID:

I'm gonna make him an offer he can't refuse.
—*Don Vito Corleone*

One thing to be avoided in employee discipline is deal making. This lowers the process to that of plea bargaining. You will be pressured by the employee association or union to do this, and even your agency's attorney may suggest it. Some department heads agree to it to avoid a lengthy hearing process or possible unfavorable publicity.

This should not be done. If the employee's action was serious enough to warrant discipline, it should be initiated and corrective active and appropriate punishment instituted.

If the offense is so serious that it requires dismissal, separate the employee immediately by placing him or her on administrative leave. Many times your controlling agency will not want you to do this, because if reinstated, the employee will receive back pay for the time missed. The agency believes it is better to keep them working than to pay them for sitting home and later collecting pay should the dismissal be overturned.

Placing the employee in a bean-counting administrative assignment should be avoided as their attitude will not be the best and they will seek sympathy and disparage management.

Next to catastrophically losing an officer, firing one is probably the most traumatic personnel issue that you will be faced with as a manager. You are emotionally attached to most of your employees even if you don't personally know them, because of the law enforcement bond. For the most part, you have been where they have been, seen what they have seen, and except for this instance, pretty much done what they have done. You feel somewhat betrayed and let down that a fellow officer would commit the offense that he did.

The department head, not you, most likely made the final decision to separate the employee, but it may have been on your recommendation.

Even if you weren't a part of the actual internal investigation, you are affected because it's happening, and it is an extremely negative occurrence for the entire organization.

Your responsibility is to make sure that the other employees in the command are provided with all of the information that it is legal to divulge. To stifle rumors, transparency is a must. It is not unusual for fellow officers to feel sympathy for the accused, which makes it important that actual facts are made known so that the department will not be falsely accused or blamed.

SOMEONE ONCE SAID:

Most people want to avoid pain, and discipline is usually painful.
—John C. Maxwell

A completely different approach to discipline, termed "positive discipline," is gaining some popularity.

It was developed by industrial psychologist **John Huberman** and is described in an article he wrote for the *Harvard Business Review* entitled "Discipline Without Punishment." Huberman's claim is that the positive discipline method puts the responsibility for correct behavior on the employee, not the employer. In essence, he was saying that the traditional method of discipline is "parental," in that it treats employees like children who must either behave or be punished.

The discipline without punishment or positive discipline method has several steps:

1. Informal Oral Reminder. If misbehavior is noted, the manager discusses the problem with the employee informally and attempts to gain a commitment to resolve the problem. The supervisor documents the problem and discussion in a private file.
2. Oral Reminder. If there is no improvement, a second discussion is held, and the tone is more serious. The incident and discussion are documented in an official file.
3. Written Reminder. If the problem persists or the misbehavior is repeated, a formal corrective memorandum is issued to the employee. This is called a "reminder" of what type of behavior is expected. It contains an improvement action plan.
4. Decision-Making Leave. If the discussions haven't produced the desired results, and the improvement plan is not working, the employee is given a day off with pay and directed to consider the wish to comply with agency directives or seek alternative employment. If the employee decides to return, goals are set and an action plan is developed. Failure to abide by the agreement will result in immediate termination.

The author emphasizes that positive discipline is corrective, not punitive. Management is no longer the bad guy, and employees are treated as adults responsible for their own behavior. They are offered the choice and the opportunity to improve and assisted in doing so.

Apparently, some three hundred organizations are using this go-home-and-think-about-it philosophy, including General Electric, American Telephone and Telegraph, Procter & Gamble, and Union Carbide.

SOMEONE ONCE SAID:

There is a difference between discipline and punishment. Punishment is what you do to someone; discipline is what you do for someone.

—Zig Ziglar

Should a department want to implement the positive discipline approach, substantial planning and coordination with human resources units would be necessary, as well as agreements obtained from unions or employee organizations. And most certainly, the "positive discipline" approach must be limited to minor offences, *which would also have to be negotiated.*

PROBLEM SOLVING

In your current position you are sure to encounter, or will have handed to you, some kind of a problem that needs solving. It can run the gamut from insignificance to deadly serious. Its solution can be obvious or unknown.

In either case, an attempt to solve the problem must be made.

SOMEONE ONCE SAID:

If I had an hour to solve a problem, I'd spend 55 minutes thinking about the problem and 5 minutes thinking about solutions.
—Albert Einstein

In the 1950s, **Taiichi Ohno**, considered to be the father of the production system at the Toyota Motor Company, striving to solve a production problem, developed a strategy called the "5 Whys."

Simply put, the process amounts to asking and answering "why" to five questions. It is described in his book *Workplace Management*.

The 5 Whys is an interrogative technique used to explore the relationships of a problem by attempting to determine its underlying cause by simply asking why. Each answer forms the basis for the next question.

The process begins by forming a group of people who have knowledge of the circumstances around which the problem occurred. They then examine what happened by utilizing the progressive 5 Whys method. This questioning of the basic reasons for the happening may not actually solve the problem, but it permits countermeasures to be put in place so that it doesn't recur.

For example:

ONCE UPON A TIME,
a murder trial was starting and the district attorney requested the police agency whose case it was to send over the murder weapon, a revolver, that purportedly was used in the crime. The homicide had taken place two years previously and the case was just coming to trial. A search of the department's evidence box for the case did not produce the gun. It had originally been logged in, but it was now missing. Next, the entire evidence storage room was searched, but the gun was not located.

The lieutenant in charge of evidence storage called together a group of employees, whose jobs somewhat involved evidence procurement and storage, and began the 5 Whys process. He started with the basic question, answered it, and then questioned the answer:

1. Why can't we find the weapon? Because it is not there.
2. Why isn't it there? It was logged in and is missing because it has been removed.
3. Why was it removed? Perhaps for the preliminary hearing. If so, why wasn't it returned?
4. Why wasn't it returned? The deputy DA knowing he would need it later did not return it, but kept it for the trial.
5. Why didn't we know this? Because we don't have a good evidence-tracking system.

What the 5 Whys team discovered was that while the department had a good system for initially logging in the evidence, it only kept track of that intake and its final disposition. If it was removed temporarily for some reason, this was not recorded. The remover was instructed to return it, and it was assumed that this was not done.

The department quickly revised its evidence-recording procedure so that future problems of the type would not occur.

Although this is a simplistic example of the 5 Why technique, it does illustrate its use and value. The asking of five questions is not a hard-and-fast rule. It may take fewer or more questions to arrive at the answer. Toyota still uses Ohno's 5 Why method for solving problems.

MEETINGS

One of the most valuable tools in problem solving is to hold meetings as suggested by Dr. Ohno. Additionally, meetings are in fact excellent management tools to propose new programs, obtain feedback, make necessary change, or sometimes just offer an opportunity to get to know one another better. But meetings do affect efficiency. Both positively and negatively. They can provide instant solutions through group problem solving or be a huge waste of time.

SOMEONE ONCE SAID:

**Don't hold a $100 meeting
to solve a $10 problem.**
—Anonymous

One of the first things to consider when planning a meeting is whether it is absolutely necessary. Remember, time is valuable. You and the attendees may have better things to do. Also, it is a pretty well-accepted fact that nobody likes meetings very much.

Meetings should be planned. Again, the old crime-solving meme of who? what? where? and why? is the place to begin when you design the gathering.

Once these are considered, and a meeting is determined to be necessary, a formal agenda is the next priority. This will serve to keep you on track, as frequently discussions can wander.

Sometimes just through the preparation for the meeting, answers to the problem may come to you and eliminate the necessity of holding it.

Amusingly, with regard to meetings,

SOMEONE ONCE SAID:

If you are lonely and don't like working alone or have trouble making decisions, then call a meeting!

You can see people!

Draw flowcharts!

Feel important!

Form subcommittees!

Impress your colleagues!

Make recommendations!

Meetings are the practical alternative to work!

—Anonymous

In other words, be absolutely sure that the reason for the meeting is clear and its purpose valid. Time is valuable!

FINALLY

The position of middle manager is truly difficult. The problems of first-line operation rise to your level and those from top management seem to drop daily into your in-basket. You are clearly where what's happened and what's going to happen meet. Both are waiting for you to do something.

If nothing else, be proud that you are certainly in the "center" of your agency's operation.

Even though you may be competent and comfortable in your mid-management position, if the opportunity to promote or perhaps move to another agency where you would be in charge comes along, you are encouraged to give it a try. You already possess the necessary management skills and have no doubt already been actively engaged in what those positions call "leadership."

SOMEONE ONCE SAID:

**Management is doing things right,
leadership is doing the right thing.**
—Peter F. Drucker

LEADERSHIP

Again, congratulations. Through the civil service system, competitive interview, political appointment, or election, you have now made it to or near the top of the organization. You and a few others will be in charge of the direction and successful operation of the organization. Your responsibilities have no doubt increased at least tenfold.

SOMEONE ONCE SAID:

Uneasy lies the head that wears the crown.
—*William Shakespeare*

TAKING COMMAND

Department or agency heads and their immediate subordinates can either rise up through the ranks from within the organization or be hired or elected and come from the outside. Both paths have their benefits and problems.

Top managers coming from within the organization should have a pretty clear picture of the strengths and weaknesses of the department. Plus, they have the advantage of knowing the same qualities in the personnel they will be supervising and working with.

Conversely, for department heads coming from the outside, the lack of this organizational knowledge is a definite handicap. This can be overcome by taking things slow for the first few weeks or months and observing and becoming acquainted with the people and the operation. The benefit of having leaders come from another agency is that they often bring fresh ideas and programs with them and are not stifled by the existing culture and doing "what we've always done."

Whichever your case, once in place, an important first step is to attempt to interview your predecessor. That individual can provide you with insight and valuable information that is unattainable anywhere else.

He or she has traveled the road and knows where the hills and valleys are located, as well as the bumps and washouts. They are familiar with the processes, programs, and people. They can help you avoid initial mistakes.

SOMEONE ONCE SAID:

Is there anyone so wise as to learn by the experience of others?
—Voltaire

If you are promoted or appointed from within the organization, your performance must have been reasonably effective at the lower ranks. Your job now is to continue that effectiveness.

There is, however, a difference. Previously you were just a part of the organization, most likely having an integral role in attempting to make it successful. Now the ultimate success of the entire organization is up to you. The credit or the blame is yours. Those same processes of management discussed at the supervisor and management levels haven't changed, but now they must be viewed and undertaken in a different manner. Your actions and decisions carry tremendous responsibility and result in meaningful outcomes.

Even though you are no longer directly involved in the ground-level day-to-day operation of the agency, it is you who must monitor compliance with the policies, rules, and regulations that determine the direction the organization takes.

SOMEONE ONCE SAID:

You have to learn the rules of the game, and then you have to play better than anyone else.
—Albert Einstein

Quite likely the department has an operational culture established by past experience and existing practices. You must now either live with it or make change.

SOMEONE ONCE SAID:

**The greater thing is not where we stand,
but where we are going.**
—*Thomas Jefferson*

Even though you are familiar with and generally in agreement with the operational guidelines in effect, take another look at them. Quite often they appear different when viewed from above rather than from below.

Does the purpose statement reflect the actual mission of the department? Does it spell out a meaningful vision? Is it taking the department where you want it to go? Is it written in understandable terms that both employees and the public will buy into?

In many cases, these written tomes are rarely looked at and just carried forward generation after generation, leader after leader.

The same is often true of general orders or written policies. New ones are added, some are amended, but most just remain in the book, rarely if ever looked at. The only exception might be when individuals are studying for a promotional exam. It is imperative that operational orders and policies be reviewed and updated at least annually.

SOMEONE ONCE SAID:

**If you always do what you've always done,
you'll always get what you've always gotten.**
—*Tony Robbins*

Even more important, one of the first things that you must do is to take a look at the personnel surrounding you, particularly those in the upper level of the organization. They will be interfacing with or reporting to you directly and frequently.

At the lower levels in the organization, staffing is primarily concerned with numbers and skills. However, at the executive level, there are other considerations.

Once you become familiar enough with your position and its requirements, you can determine what type and how many close assistants you will need. Larger departments may require a management team while others can get by with an assistant chief or undersheriff at the executive level.

This can be more adequately determined by answering the following: At the executive level:

- What actually needs to be done?
- Are there sufficient resources available to accomplish it?
- Are the employees in place skilled enough to accomplish what is necessary?
- How much am I willing to delegate?

For the most part, if the organization is operating at an acceptable level, minor noted deficiencies can be corrected at a later date. Take your time in making a major overhaul of the department, for you may be stuck with some of the errors you make.

LEADERSHIP

In his book *Motivation in the Real World*, respected author and management guru **Saul Gellerman** cautioned, "If no one is following, you're not leading." He went on to say that if you are having an influence on someone else's behavior and that influence causes the person to act as you want, you are exercising leadership. However, if your actions have no or a negative effect on what other people do, you are not leading. What he was saying is that a job title or position does not make you a leader. It is how you carry out the responsibilities of that position that determine whether or not you a leader.

SOMEONE ONCE SAID:

The boss drives his men;
the leader coaches them.

The boss depends upon authority;
the leader on good will.

The boss inspires fear;
the leader inspires enthusiasm.

The boss says "I";
the leader says "we."

The boss fixes blame for the breakdown;
the leader fixes the breakdown.

The boss says "go";
the leader says "let's go!"
—*H. Gordon Selfridge*

Adding to that,

SOMEONE ONCE SAID:

**Leadership is what gives an organization
its vision and its ability to translate
that vision into reality.**
—Warren Bennis

And in his book (co-authored with **Burt Nanus**) *Leaders: The Strategies for Taking Charge,*

BENNIS ALSO SAID:

**Many organizations are over managed
and under led.**

You are now at or approaching or have reached the peak or highest identified level of Abraham Maslow's hierarchy, that of self-actualization, and you are enjoying the success of accomplishment and "being the best you can be."

What is this quality or ability called leadership, where does it come from, and how do we get it if we don't have it?

In 1856, **Charles Darwin**, the English naturalist and biologist, proposed his evolutionary theory of "natural selection." He believed that for a species to survive, the strongest members of that species reproduce, passing on their superior qualities and abilities. Those not so strong pass on a lesser set of inheritances and in some cases may not reproduce or survive.

It seems a stretch to be discussing Darwinism with the subject of leadership, but throughout history, in discussions of societal makeup, it has been claimed that those who rise to the top have inborn qualities or traits that single them out for the role of leader.

It was this belief that gave birth to monarchy. If a king was a great leader, it would follow that his son, the prince, would also make a great king. Thus, whether the royals were deserving or not, governance of the realm was passed down through generations of them. Those not having "royal" blood were destined to be followers.

The Leadership Quarterly, a multidisciplinary social science journal dedicated to the study of leadership, recently reported on ongoing technical studies conducted by the National Longitudinal Study of Adolescent Health. The purpose of the study was to determine whether there is such a thing as a natural-born leader, or in the researchers' words, "Do humans have an innate predisposition to occupy a leadership role?" or "Are some humans naturally selected to be leaders?" Similar to what Darwin espoused.

The researchers made their determination through the study of genes. Their findings reveal that the heritability of leadership genes is 24 percent. Simply put, leadership qualities can be partially inherited.

Another researcher, Terry "Starbucker" St. Marie, a recognized business and management consultant, strategist, and blogger, claims that great leaders possess characteristics that they are born with, making them natural-born leaders. He lists the following ten qualities that define a natural leader:

1. Courtesy: the ability to simply express your respect or gratitude by using words like "please" or "thank you"
2. Generosity: the willingness to devote time, effort, and patience toward colleagues, without expecting anything in return
3. Humility: putting the welfare of others before yours
4. Empathy: putting yourself in the shoes of others
5. Consideration: having a genuine regard and concern toward others
6. Courage: the ability to make difficult decisions and take risks
7. Compassion: the concern for the suffering of others and wanting to see that suffering end
8. Integrity: a commitment or will to do the right thing
9. Civility: having good manners
10. Contrition: the ability to admit mistakes and apologize

St. Marie is certainly correct with regard to identifying ten critical and important management qualities. As he postulates, even if one is not born with them, they are certainly virtues that you can acquire and practice. Some of these will later be discussed.

As with most things, there is usually an opposing view.

SOMEONE ONCE SAID:

Leaders are made, they are not born. They are made by hard effort, which is the price we must pay to achieve a worthwhile goal.
—Vince Lombardi

It is now accepted that the attributes of leadership can be learned and acquired. This is accomplished through education and experience. Even though it may not be in your blood, to have reached your present position, you have shown that you possess leadership ability. Now you must use it.

LEADERSHIP PHILOSOPHIES

One of your initial considerations when assuming command of the organization is to examine it and try to determine just what type of management style it is currently engaged in. If you were promoted or appointed from within, you are already aware of it. The question then is do you want to or need to make a change? Quite often, new leaders make material, operational, and staffing changes, but they overlook examination of the philosophical thoughts and behaviors of the agency.

The current leadership philosophy and style may be working fine and may have been established through inheritance or just evolution into what was comfortable for your predecessor, but it may not be yours. If you are uncomfortable with it, you should change it.

Merriam-Webster's defines leadership as "the action of leading people or an organization." It defines leadership philosophy as "a theory or attitude that acts as a guiding principle for a leader's behavior."

Combining the two provides a general description of the theory of leadership. It consists of an overall system of beliefs and actions on the part of management that guide and control the direction of the organization.

It is your beliefs, principles, values, attitudes, and expectations that form your leadership philosophy. And it is that philosophy that provides direction for you and the organization.

SOMEONE ONCE SAID:

An organization will take on the personality of its leader.
—Abraham Lincoln

Following are leadership styles that you have no doubt been exposed to, some of which you may be using:

- Laissez-faire leadership professes that subordinates should have the power to make decisions. If they are capable and knowledgeable, this can work. You must, however, have a casual approach to management and not concern yourself with the details.

- Democratic leadership believes that through cooperation, participation, and giving consideration to the contribution of the subordinates in decision making, organizational success will be achieved. This model is currently used by many successful organizations.

- Autocratic leadership is where the leader makes decisions and has an independent vision of how things should be accomplished in a controlled environment. This is pretty much the leadership philosophy of the military, and it is effective. It can be instituted to overcome a chaotic condition if one has been allowed to develop.

- Inspirational leadership is an "employees-come-first" style, where their interests and development are most important to management. It is expected that they will respond by becoming loyal and hardworking in order to live up to the administration's expectations.

- Results-based leadership believes that getting the job done quickly and efficiently is all important. Results and achievement of goals are the most important operational factors. The use of goals can be included in other philosophies.

- Collaborative leadership is an even more employee-involved style of management than the democratic style. Instead of just soliciting input from the employees, management has them actively engaged in the running of the organization.

- Example-setting leadership depends on your actions always being near perfect. The organizational environment you set is successful, making your actions desirable and worthy of being copied. This element should be present no matter which leadership method or style is adopted.
- Strategic leadership is where the day-to-day management of the mundane and minute details of the operation is left for others to do. This type of leader devotes interest and energy to the bottom line or outcome. In military thinking, concentration is on winning the war, not worrying about the battles.
- Affiliative leadership gets down in the trenches with the employees and is an actual part of the working team. This type of behavior inspires loyalty to both the organization and the leader, as employees view the leader as an ally. Unfortunately, quite often the "big picture" is overlooked due to overconcentration on the day-to-day operation.
- Charismatic leadership depends on the leader developing a personal relationship with employees so that they will work diligently so as to not displease or let him down. In larger organizations this is accomplished by frequent conversational videotapes or Zoom-type conferences.

All of these models have value, and all are in use to some extent in most organizations.

What you should now determine is which, if any, you want to personally adopt and implement in your agency. One more than the others may fit your personality, and you may be more comfortable using that one.

Management experts recommend that rather than exclusively adopting one of the styles, leaders should instead use them in combination and sometimes situationally. For example, if a situation is volatile or critical, perhaps a laissez-faire or collaborative style should be replaced temporarily by the more autocratic style.

The Union's Civil War hero, General Ulysses Grant, apparently did this. In the book *Cigars, Whiskey and Winning: Leadership Lessons from Ulysses S. Grant*, **Al Kaltman** describes how Grant learned to become a great leader by serving under Generals Winfield Scott and Zachary Taylor in the Mexican War. These two differed greatly in their approach to leadership. General Taylor reportedly took a relaxed, almost laissez-faire approach, rarely wearing a uniform or paying attention to protocol. General Scott was the complete opposite, being extremely officious and formal in his bearing. Always in a complete and impeccable uniform. Always the General! Yet both were successful commanders and leaders.

Grant admired both and was appreciative of the leadership skills and knowledge he learned, although different, from each. He learned that there were times when informality worked and other times when an autocratic style was necessary.

In adopting and using a leadership style, you should adopt the one style or combination of those styles that you are most comfortable with. But remember that your true focus should be its effectiveness rather than your personal comfort with a particular style.

Earlier the characteristics of flexibility and consistency and their influence on operations and outcomes were discussed. At this level, too, they must be considered. Consistency in a leadership style is important, but the door for flexibility should be left open.

PERSONAL LEADERSHIP PHILOSOPHY

Many experts are now making the claim that to succeed as a leader, in addition to an organizational leadership philosophy, you *must* have a "personal leadership philosophy," or PLP.

The PLP is a formal declaration that consists of your beliefs, values, and those things in life that are the most important to you.

The authorities recommend that the PLP be in writing as this serves to convince you that you are making a serious commitment to this philosophy, that it will remain consistent, and that it amounts to more than random thoughts. Plus, it is available for review and can be updated and shared if so desired.

Formulation of your personal leadership philosophy is accomplished in much the same way you designed the leadership philosophy of the agency. It outlines for you your personal beliefs and values and, once those are identified, provides direction for your career and life.

W. Rolfe Kerr, an emeritus general authority of The Church of Jesus Christ of Latter-day Saints (LDS), has published a PLP or, as he expressed it, a "personal creed." It offers an example of what your PLP might include. The following is paraphrased and does not include Kerr's religious urgings:

I will;
Never compromise with honesty
Hear both sides before judging
Plan tomorrow's work today
Defend those who are absent

Maintain a positive attitude
Facilitate the success of subordinates
Be sincere yet decisive
Concentrate all abilities and efforts on the
task at hand
Listen twice as much as I speak
Not fear mistakes
Care about my people
—*W. Rolfe Kerr*

Stephen R. Covey gave credit to W. Rolfe Kerr's thoughts and recommended that every leader develop what he termed a "personal mission statement." Covey's is very similar Kerr's but also includes:

Develop one new proficiency per year
Hustle while you wait
Be orderly in person and work
Keep a sense of humor
Obtain counsel of others

These are general and individual principles to live and lead by. They can be added to, subtracted from, or personalized. Develop and formalize your own Personal leadership philosophy or personal mission statement, refer to it, and follow it.

BUILD TEAMS

Keith Davis, again in *Human Behavior at Work: Human Relations*, recommends that an organization have two types of teams. One should be made up of the entire organization where the members have mutual interests and goals and believe in the success of the group. Let's hope your department has such a team. Fortunately, most law enforcement agencies do.

Operational teams are the second type. These teams are formed by employees having similar jobs and responsibilities. They are your different units, sections, squads, shifts, and so on that work closely together in activities generally termed "teamwork."

For the most part, these teams are cohesive and made up of developed friendships. They have common purpose and goals, and the individuals trust and depend on each other in their day-to-day operations. Even if there may be some friction between members, the good of the group usually wins out. The belief may be "we are all in the same boat, and no one is going to sink us." Management should encourage these types of teams as long as their desires and actions are positive.

These operational groups consist of the majority of the department's employees. In most cases, because of civil service regulations or union contracts, they will remain. Therefore, it is essential that you garner their assistance and support. You have to get them to trust and have confidence in you.

Initially, some employees may show indifference to you while others may be more overt and display nonacceptance or even hostility.

You should understand that for the most part, expressions of dislike or disrespect are generally not aimed at you personally. It is human nature to be suspicious of and resist change, and you are change.

Or perhaps, employees had had a favorite or a friend whom they wanted to head the department, and you getting the job upset that plan.

The people who may initially resist you can be at every level. Although persons of a lesser rank or non-sworn personnel may not have the influence of those higher in the organization, through creation of subtle disruption and resistance, they can slow down your plans and make life more difficult for you.

While they are judging you, you must also judge them and assure yourself that they are a qualified workforce. In a smaller agency or command, you should review their personnel files and performance reports and make personal contact with them.

SOMEONE ONCE SAID:

Bad attitudes will ruin your team.
—Terry Bradshaw

Attitude correction is not so simple. This is where the supervisory and management skills you have acquired through experience and training pay off. It is accomplished by establishing a positive worker-friendly environment as taught by McGregor, McClelland, and the others and by adopting a constructive leadership philosophy.

The Navy SEALs, as do the elite groups of the other military forces, pride themselves on their team concept of management and organization. They have extremely high selection standards and intense training criteria, where less than exemplary attitude and performance are grounds for removal. An individual's skills are important, but the functioning of the team is paramount. As **Robert Needham**'s *Team Secrets of the Navy Seals* repeatedly stresses, "You fail as a team, or succeed as a team!" Common goals are a must, and the team is only as good as its weakest member.

These same beliefs can be utilized in building your overall organizational team, or in encouraging and supporting individual groups or work teams within the department. First-line supervisors are very important in creating and continuing the effectiveness and efficiency of these teams.

Deficiencies in knowledge and/or skills can normally be overcome by training. Morale problems can usually be overcome by adoption and implementation of a more participative management style reflecting McGregor's Theory Y approach.

LEADERSHIP TEAM

Notwithstanding Keith Davis's recommendation that organizations have two teams, there is a compelling need for still another team.

This team is vitally important! It is a "leadership team." Your leadership team.

Virtually every leader relies on a group of trusted individuals for support, advice, and assistance in completing the mission. This is the group that you will spend most of your work time with. These individuals will report directly to you, and you will be their direct supervisor.

SOMEONE ONCE SAID:

If you want to go fast, go alone.
If you want to go far, go together.
—*African proverb*

To have such a team, you must surround yourself with personnel who are capable, motivated, and supportive not only of the organization but of you personally. This may be more difficult than earning the confidence of the agency as a whole.

As soon as you can, upon assuming your new position, hold a general meeting with the staff members whom you will be working most closely with. This will give you the opportunity to explain your philosophies, expectations, and so on.

Following this, arrange to meet one-on-one with that staff. These meetings can be formal or informal. Your primary objective is to get to know them if you don't already and to have them get to know you.

Find out about their family, their interests, and their work history and career objectives. At the same time, share all of the above about you with them. The results of these interactions may determine what your next steps are.

These initial interactions should give you knowledge of their strengths and weaknesses. If their weak areas can't be corrected through training or restructuring their responsibilities, you must consider replacing them.

Even more important, they must be on your side. Their management philosophies, traits, and temperaments don't have to exactly mirror yours, but they must be compatible. Plus, their confidence and belief in your and the agency's goals are vital. They must recognize and respect the fact that you are the "boss."

By this stage in your career, your ability to recognize the signs of discontent should be in place.

In your leadership group are there individuals who consistently question your decisions? Do they appear reluctant to follow your directions? Or do they tacitly resist implementing changes that you want to make?

Generally, this resistance will be surreptitious rather than overt. Taking action on your orders or requests may be put off or delayed.

Your directives may be passed down in an unclear or even demanding manner so as to upset the recipients. Any act creating dissatisfaction within the agency, although not overtly, will be blamed on you.

Reasons and excuses will be made for all of these actions. Initially, you should appear understanding, but you must take corrective steps.

Meet with the identified individuals or group, explain your side of any issue, and solicit input about their thoughts and concerns.

You should advise any still-recalcitrant individuals, nonconfrontationally, on your need for their cooperation and support. You should make clear that it is not in their best interest to fight the system and that you plan on being there for a long time. What about them?

Can't we just all get along?
—Rodney King

If by exercising the positive management practices that have previously been discussed you become known as a fair leader, opinions may change.

Coming together is a beginning,
Keeping together is progress.
Working together is success.
—Henry Ford

Building teams is absolutely necessary; most importantly, so is building your leadership team.

It is essential that you realize that loyalty is a two-way street, and any trust that you expect to receive must be given in return, usually even more so. That is why it is such an important element in any administration, particularly in your leadership team.

An important consideration is that during your absence, one of the team members will be in command and running the department. For that reason alone, you must have complete trust in them and confidence in their abilities.

If not, some type of corrective or replacement action must be taken.

Sometimes transfer of an individual can be accomplished. Simple rearrangement of their duties is another course of action that can be taken.

Effective leadership is putting first things first.
—Stephen R. Covey

If you observe that you and your team are for the most part on the same page philosophically, your future is much easier. If not, you have some choices to make and actions to take.

Since first becoming an officer, you have known that decision making was one of the skills that you had to develop. Realistically, it was earlier in your career that you were faced with far more important and critical decisions than these personnel issues. Arrest or not? Shoot? Don't shoot?

Apparently, in those instances you must have decided correctly, or else you would not have achieved this level in the organization.

Perhaps in this situation, the easiest thing to do is nothing. Can you live with their differences in opinion, management styles, basic philosophies, or personalities?

Sometimes this is possible, but it is rarely the best solution.

SOMEONE ONCE SAID:

**In any moment of decision the best thing
you can do is the right thing.
The worst thing you can do is nothing.**
—Theodore Roosevelt

There are some alternative approaches that you can attempt. One is to hold another meeting where you again explain, in more detail, your same goals and desires for the organization and how the support of management is critical in achieving success. Try to get the group to agree and to buy in.

Or perhaps you can use those who are reacting positively to your plan to bring along their peers. Sometimes the individual's belonging need, as identified by Maslow, will be enough to change an attitude.

Another option might be to provide training that outlines your beliefs or thoughts on the areas not being accepted. You may even want to send particular individuals to specific training on particular subjects.

Also, you must be sure that *you* remain faithful and supportive of the programs and principles you are espousing!

SOMEONE ONCE SAID:

People will follow your footsteps more readily than they will follow your advice.
—William Tyndale

By this time, hopefully, most differences should be settled. If you haven't reached a resolution, you may just have to arrive at an "I am the boss and we are going to do things my way" understanding.

SOMEONE ONCE SAID:

It's my way or the highway.
—Anonymous

This is certainly not the best way to settle differences and bring people on board, but after attempting the former less drastic approaches without change or acceptance on their part, it may be necessary.

At this point, although the actions you are taking aren't considered discipline, you should be sure to document everything that has been done. This documentation may be necessary to substantiate less than favorable performance evaluations or, in the extreme, future punitive action or separation from the team.

Once you are satisfied that your team is competent and accepts your management style and vision for the agency, it is time to get to work.

LOYALTY

The essence of this discussion about building your leadership team was the necessity of gaining mutual respect, trust, and loyalty between you and your close working associates.

Superintendent **O. W. Wilson** placed high importance on the necessity of loyalty between the leaders and those being led in an organization. In his book *Police Administration*, he instructed that loyalty is a feeling or attitude resulting from an emotional rather than intellectual process, that it is based on people's feelings toward one another, and that it must go both ways. Leader to subordinate and the reverse.

SOMEONE ONCE SAID:

Loyalties are mutual in so far as our activity in carrying out our purposes helps others carry out their purposes.
—*James C. Coleman*

Superintendent Wilson's advice was consistent with what has been discussed regarding leadership. As a leader, you must develop a rapport with the workers by showing an actual interest in them and their welfare, both within and outside the organization. You accomplish this by establishing and maintaining an open-door policy and both-direction communications. You also inspire confidence by making decisions that are beneficial to both the department and the individual employees. Leaders must also strive to improve working conditions and provide recognition and reward for accomplishment.

If you can do this, according to Superintendent Wilson, your efforts will result in the workforce's repayment through improved effort, support, and loyalty.

SOMEONE ONCE SAID:

Employee loyalty begins with employer loyalty.
—Harvey Mackay

If you have established and made known your management methods and leadership philosophies, instructed your immediate staff about them, and gained their acceptance and compliance, your agency will be heading in the right direction and your job will be much easier.

As time goes by, these sentiments often progress from agency loyalty to interpersonal bonding and lasting friendships.

What you want is the kind of mutual loyalty that exists between the K-9 handler and his or her dog.

> ***Once upon a time,***
>
> in a medium-size county sheriff's department, the sheriff had been in office for several terms and was well liked and respected by the public and the members of the department. He had decided to retire and not seek reelection when his present term ended in ten months.
>
> Tragically, he was involved in an off-duty traffic accident and suffered minor brain damage. After recovery, his excellent memory returned and he was fully functional in most areas. He did, however, have trouble in reasoning and numerical expression. His physician explained this as injury to the cerebral cortex, which might or might not improve with time.
>
> The undersheriff, who had been selected by the sheriff when first elected, was one of the few people who knew of the sheriff's condition. To all others, he appeared normal, having full use of his facilities.

The undersheriff and the sheriff privately discussed the situation. The sheriff believed the only option was to retire immediately, as this would then automatically promote the undersheriff, who would serve as sheriff until the upcoming election. He hadn't entered the "race," but he could and, if he did, would most likely be reelected.

They had worked together for a long time, and the undersheriff wanted to see the sheriff complete his term and retire respectfully after fulfilling his duties. He offered to work even more closely with the sheriff for the remaining months, completing the tasks that the sheriff was no longer capable of, and telling no one. Then they would retire together.

And that is what they did.

And that is loyalty.

Hopefully during your career this type of allegiance and fidelity can be developed between you and your staff.

SOMEONE ONCE SAID:

Loyalty is not a work, it's a lifestyle.
—*Kushanwizdom Tumblr*

RELATIONSHIPS AND CARING

To get the very best out of your employees, they must believe that you care. Not just about law enforcement or the organization, but about them. **John C. Maxwell**, who is currently one of the world's most enlightened leadership mentors, in his book *The 360 Degree Leader*, lists mutual caring as one of the most important and necessary ingredients for a successful organization.

He stresses that a mutual and demonstrated concern between you and your employees is a necessary ingredient in the development of the loyalty discussed earlier.

SOMEONE ONCE SAID:

**To handle yourself, use your head,
to handle others, use your heart.**
—Eleanor Roosevelt

As a leader you must get across to your employees that you are concerned about their welfare and that you are there to assist and protect them. Not only must you convince them of this caring, you must actually believe and practice it.

ONCE UPON A TIME,
in a large department, there was a captain who commanded a district. Through no fault of his own, he had probably the worst month imaginable, both on and off the job.

First, it was learned that one of his officers was shaking down pimps and prostitutes. These street workers would be apprehended and, rather than arrested, would pay the officer for their release. Rumors of these goings-on surfaced, but they were not believed. Eventually, though, owing to the repetitiousness, a thorough investigation was conducted, the misconduct was verified, and the officer was fired. Local media coverage of the situation was fierce once it was discovered that this had been going on for some time, and it appeared that the commander had not taken the information seriously and acted on it.

On the day following the media uproar about the shakedowns, an officer on a traffic stop was hit and killed by a DUI driver. As can be imagined, this type of occurrence was exceptionally stressful for the commander, particularly since he and the officer were close, having worked together for several years.

Within a week of this happening, another officer was involved in a shooting in which the citizen was killed. The initial finding was that the shooting was not justified. Another agency was involved in the incident and was publicly critical of the officer's actions and the department's handling of the situation. The resulting uproar from the public and the accusations made by the other agency and the victim's family piled even more stress on the commander.

Following these incidents, the commander's son, who was away at college, was hospitalized after being involved in a serious automobile crash.

All of these events took place in just over a month. The commander suffered a mild stroke, definitely stress related. He went off the job and never returned.

A critical postevaluation of the agency head's actions or inactions throughout this ordeal will possibly show that maybe some demonstration of concern or care on his part might have made a difference.

The agency head, of course, had knowledge of all the events that had occurred in the commander's district.

1. Should he have considered what the commander might be experiencing emotionally?
2. Should he have been concerned enough to contact the commander and inquire about his welfare?
3. Should he have taken the time to reassure the commander that even though some of the happenings may have contained policy and procedure questions, everything would work out?
4. Did his leadership style really include caring for his employees?
5. Did others in the department notice his apparent disinterest in the commander's welfare? If so, what were their reactions?
6. Did there exist an atmosphere of openness and trust in the organization where the commander would have felt comfortable in bringing forward his personal stress or anxieties?
7. If the leader had demonstrated even a small degree of caring, might the outcome have been different?

Agreeing with John Maxwell's belief that a leader must care for his employees is easy to say, but actually doing it is an entirely different matter.

In this case, the agency head was very concerned with the incidents and what problems they created for the agency as he should have been. But he displayed little concern for the commander. Perhaps if he had, a career could have been saved. It is very easy to become so immersed in routine operational problems that a subordinate's personal distress is overlooked.

Not every leader will be faced with a situation as dreadful as described, but every leader must continually be cognizant of the need to engage in caring. Not just in words but actions.

Ways that you can show that you care:

- Get personal. Show interest in people's lives. Know a little about them, their families and interests.
- Make sure that you frequently tell them how important they are to the organization.

- Personally recognize, thank, and reward them for what they do.
- Make frequent personal interactions with them a priority.
- If they are experiencing difficulties, either job related or personal, do what you can to assist, reassure, and support them.
- Show that you care.

None of these suggestions are complex or difficult; they just need to be thought of and done! They might make a big difference in someone's career or life and will surely make a difference in the kind of leader you are.

SOMEONE ONCE SAID:

They may forget what you said, they may forget what you did, but they will never forget how you made them feel.
—*Carl W. Buecher*

Another important point! Should you ever be unfortunate enough to lose one of your employees in an on-duty death, do not forget their family. As traumatic as the experience is to you, it is at least a hundred times that to the close family. Parents, spouses, and children will be suffering greatly. So will the deceased's fellow officers.

Although it is customary to engage with the family and offer assistance and consolation immediately following the occurrence, once the funeral or "celebration of life" ceremony is over and the folded flag and badge presented to the next of kin, for the most part the department's involvement officially ends.

This should not be the case. At some point, the employee's name will no doubt be added to a "fallen officer's memorial" of some type. Make sure the family is invited to the ceremony and given dignitary status.

Also, if your agency has social gatherings, be they association or union member meetings, retiree reunions, dinners for spouses, family picnics, and so on, do what you can to have members of the deceased officer's family included in these gatherings.

SOMEONE ONCE SAID:

It is your duty as a leader and a human to go beyond the trite cliché "Our thoughts and prayers are with you."

—Author

LEADERSHIP BY NEGLECT

SOMEONE ONCE SAID:

**We never fail when we try to do our duty,
we always fail when we neglect to do it.**
—Robert Baden-Powell

So far, various philosophies and types of successful leadership styles have been discussed. There is, however, another leadership style that should be noted. It should not even be considered as a type of leadership but recognized as a system having a complete absence of that quality. This style is a couple of steps further removed than the laissez-faire philosophy. Lacking a better description, it will be termed leadership by neglect.

> *ONCE UPON A TIME,*
> there was a middle manager in a medium-size department who was about two years short of retirement. His motivation and job interest had slackened, and prospects of promotion were absent. He noticed that a small city was advertising for a chief and that the position paid slightly more than he was currently making. He really didn't want to assume the additional responsibility, but he knew that the small city department was on the same statewide retirement system he was currently under, and thinking to increase his retirement earnings, he applied for the position.

Even though his career was less than stellar, he had gone up through the ranks without any major shortfalls, and because his current chief gave a favorable recommendation (possibly because she wanted to create an opening for a more talented or industrious person), he was perhaps reluctantly hired.

At his swearing in, three new officers were also added to the department. They were replacements, not additional. They represented one-third of the force. Yet in the months following, he made no real effort to schedule or provide ride-alongs or familiarization or indoctrination training for them. His reason was that it was the academy's job to train them, not his.

The city that employed him enjoyed an ag-based economy and population and personified small-town America. Historically, except for a few petty crimes, police demands were few. More recently, though, because of a major and successful anticrime effort in a large nearby city, gangs, drugs, and homelessness had fled the pressure and were being pushed out to the smaller surrounding towns.

This township that hadn't experienced a homicide in a decade had two gang killings in the first few months of the new chief's tenure. Drug deals in broad daylight were observed on Main Street. Petty thefts and vandalism complaints increased, and the citizens attributed it to the increase of derelicts they claimed were taking over the community.

It became apparent to department members, city leaders, and the general public that something was wrong and needed fixing.

Meanwhile, the new chief was enjoying his status. He did not relocate into his new jurisdiction but commuted daily from his home some distance away. He would time his departure from home each morning precisely at the beginning of his shift and leave early enough at the end of the day to go off-duty just as he pulled into his driveway. Thus he shortened his actual work time by over an hour. He of course commuted in an official car, which occasionally deprived patrol of a needed vehicle.

He instituted no changes to policies or procedures, even though the need for reassignments and deployment alterations created by the increased crime activity made the need for change obvious.

The chief did join the statewide and local chief's associations, which necessitated that he spend time attending various meetings and functions out of the city and away from the job.

Within a short period, one of the officers who had been hired at the same time as the chief became involved in a somewhat unusual incident. While responding to a domestic situation call, he did not copy the correct address and ended up shooting a neighbor's small cocker spaniel that was barking at him as he approached the wrong house. It was no doubt poor judgment, but some believed that had he gone through an actual break-in or ride-a-long period, perhaps he might have used other tactics. The department took a lot of heat, directed mainly at the chief for failing to provide proper training to the officers. Although minor, the incident resulted in a civil suit being filed against the city.

In the third month of the chief's employment, submission of a budget was required. Even having knowledge of the dramatic increase in crime and the need for perhaps additional personnel, equipment, and certainly training, he submitted the same budget as was prepared and submitted by the former chief the previous year. Plus, he detailed a sergeant to attend the budget hearing.

As might be expected, the mayor, the town council, and the public were becoming upset and exasperated. It appeared to them, correctly so, that management of the police department was lacking. It seemed that nothing was being done to stem the increasing crime situation in their city.

When brought before the council, the chief declared that he was doing a fine job. His defense regarding the crime issues was that he was doing everything he could, but because the department had to compete with the larger agencies in the surrounding cities that paid more for personnel, he could not hire the best officers and was stuck with less qualified personnel. These "bottom-of-the-barrel" individuals were largely unmotivated and only marking time until they could get a job with another agency.

Once this pronouncement became known within the department, morale was adversely affected, and what little motivation had been present disappeared.

During the next couple of months, no improvement in any area was made and the chief was fired. The state sent in law enforcement assistance to try to manage the crime situation, giving the city time to reorganize its police department.

This example clearly illustrates the philosophy of "leadership by neglect" and its implications. Not only was the city forced to endure the increase in crime, it was forced to once again go through the hiring process to replace the chief. Unfortunately, this chief's actions, or lack of them, reflected badly on the city, the department, the police profession, and more precisely on law enforcement leadership.

It has been recognized by every management authority that competent leadership is one of the most valuable qualities for an organization to possess. Even marginal leadership is requisite.

SOMEONE ONCE SAID:

The quality of the result is directly proportional to the quality of the leadership.
—Author

Now that you are in charge, it is imperative that you not relax your efforts and determination to make the department one to be proud of.

As a start, consider the manner in which the chief in the example led, then do the opposite. You cannot neglect your personnel, your responsibilities, or fixing that which is broken.

SOMEONE ONCE SAID:

It is the neglect of timely repair that makes rebuilding necessary.
—Richard Whately

BUREAUCRACY

Although maybe not obvious, you were in your previous positions involved in the official internal workings and dealings of the organization. These were not the structure and duties depicted on the organizational chart, but they were just as important in getting the job done.

Rarely formalized into directives, every organization has unofficial rules, or often just strict understandings of how things must be done. These mechanisms guide the operation of the institution. They are highly regimented often to the point of absurdity but certainly real. This reality is known as the bureaucracy.

SOMEONE ONCE SAID:

Bureaucracy makes the possible, impossible.
—Javier Pasqual

Max Weber, a German sociologist and author, was the first to coin the term "bureaucracy." He identified it as an organizational structure that is characterized by many both written and unwritten rules, standardized processes, procedures, and requirements. This behavioral control consists of a strict hierarchy and meticulous division of labor and responsibility.

Further, all regular activities within the bureaucracy can be regarded as official duties.

He theorized that management because of its divine right and superior knowledge has the authority and responsibility to impose rules and, further, that these rules must be followed because they are based on established and proven methods and procedures.

Weber's idea of management emphasized the division of labor, a controlling hierarchy, and rules with virtually no interpersonal relationships. Directives had to be followed because management knows best. And not every rule in a bureaucratic system has to be written down, but it must be followed.

> Example: Everyone knows and understands that a sergeant is in control of the officers and that his or her rule is supreme and should not be questioned. Yet in most agencies, this is just an understanding and not really written down anywhere. A chain of command may indicate it, but even if not, it is an absolute and obeyed bureaucratic rule.

According to Weber, the advantage of establishing and applying a formal and unswerving "bureaucratic" approach was that it made for efficient management and established formal control and consistent work by the employees. Douglas McGregor and Frederick Taylor must have studied Weber's bureaucracy concept while developing their Theory X and Taylorism beliefs.

While seemingly a negative approach to management, the bureaucratic theory was identified and accepted as a must-have management principle in 1905, and surprisingly, it is still in use in many successful organizations.

The obvious disadvantages are that it consists of many layers of red tape and large amounts of paperwork, and it encourages disloyalty because of its formality and lack of interpersonal relations.

As a new arrival at the leadership level, you are encouraged to examine the workings of your organization and determine whether it fits into Weber's model.

Recent management studies have begun to question the real value of bureaucracy. Tom Peters, again in *Thriving on Chaos*, attacks bureaucracy as an enemy of modern management. He claims that it is "a block to survival" of the organization. And its reduction "is a strategic priority of the first order."

Work expands to fill the allotted time.
—*C. Northcote Parkinson*

The above quote was taken from *Parkinson's Law: The Pursuit of Progress*, a book written by **C. Northcote Parkinson**. The book was based on his experience with the British Civil Service. His thesis was that bureaucracies grow, whether or not their responsibilities change. He observed that officials (leaders) want to multiply the number of their subordinates and that they make work simply to justify the expansions.

These were apparently scientific observations supported by a mathematical equation proving the growth of a bureaucracy, some 5 to 7 percent per year, with no change in the jobs or responsibilities. The only change was the additional number of people needed to accomplish them. And this need was brought about by instituting additional rules and regulations and unnecessary controls and by increasing the bureaucracy.

One argument Parkinson made, which was later termed the "triviality law," was that bureaucracies spend too much time on trivial issues. He used as an example a committee that was charged with construction of a nuclear power plant. It spent an inordinate amount of time discussing the construction of an attendant bicycle shed, rather than the primary task of building the plant itself. This bureaucratic diversion is popularly called bike-shedding and unfortunately takes place in many agencies.

ONCE UPON A TIME,
the newly appointed chief of a large department had been requested to provide security for the president of the United States during an upcoming visit to her city. She sent a directive to the planning unit to develop a plan for the mission.

The department had previously provided the same type of security for the president, so she was provided with the previous plan. It was a simple document that consisted of coordinating with the president's Secret Service detail about the time, place, duration of the event, the travel route, and so on. Once those details were learned, the number of personnel necessary and their assignments were included.

The chief returned it to the planning unit, specifying more detail was needed. For instance, what was the uniform of the day, what additional weapons, if any, would be carried, possible overtime costs, and so on. She even wondered if the officers should be polled to determine whether their political beliefs were the same as the president's.

The planned visit was to be in fifteen days, and during that period the entire Planning Unit was occupied with the proposal. It was forwarded to the chief four times and each time was returned for changes and more detail. One particular direction that was unpopular was that when the president's car passed by officers on fixed post, they were to come to attention, salute, and remain so until the vehicle passed. When it was learned that the first lady might accompany the president, the plan had to have an almost total revision. No weapons other than the normal duty weapons could be displayed. Motorcycles, because of their noise and offensive fumes, shouldn't be close to the FLOTUS, and most officers in immediate contact with the presidential party should be female.

The final bureaucratic document consisted of more than forty pages and so irritated someone that it was leaked to the media.

Both the public and the city council became interested. The interest centered on the extensiveness and cost of the plan and its undertaking. The interest heightened and turned somewhat negative toward the department when the visit was canceled at the last minute. It was not the president's fault; a declared weather emergency in another part of the country claimed his attendance.

"Wasteful!" was the leadoff in media coverage. "What was the chief thinking? So much for so little." For nothing actually.

Try to not let a bureaucratic urge lead you astray.

SOMEONE ONCE SAID:

Misdirected focus on paperwork, on procedures, and on bureaucracy frustrates everyone and must be avoided.
—Author

The US Army has 542 field manuals instructing on everything from how to conduct drills and ceremonies to setting and disarming booby traps. Most of these are never referenced, but they are there, sitting on a shelf somewhere. Rarely if ever are they updated. Just recently, however, the army did revise its primary combat manuals that deal with large-scale ground combat operations, last used in the 1970s, to discuss deploying smaller counterinsurgent forces. If a giant bureaucracy like the army finds it necessary to occasionally examine its operation, perhaps you should too.

SOMEONE ONCE SAID:

Bureaucracy defends the status quo long past the time when the quo has lost its status.
—Laurence J. Peter

Something to consider as you study your department might be that perhaps a personnel audit may be necessary. To suggest a reduction in personnel immediately following your assumption of command would certainly be unpopular, but perhaps as positions become vacant, the necessity of refilling them should be evaluated.

Also, question if ongoing or proposed projects are really necessary. Are they contributing to the achievement of the agency's purpose and goals?

Similar to the presidential visit fiasco, the media recently went to great lengths to describe and criticize the efforts of a local department's wanting to improve community relations by repainting its vehicles a light blue color to lessen the aggressive image of the traditional black-and-whites. The media called it "bureaucratic nonsense!" and asked, "Why don't you just train your officers to be nicer?"

Question if your department has rules and regulations that are restrictive and confining to an unnecessary level. Many times they came about because in the past, someone committed an act that was not approved by management. Then, no matter how minuscule, insignificant, or rare the act, if ever done, someone in management took the "shotgun" corrective approach by making a written rule prohibiting the act. This could have been done decades ago, but the rule is still in the book.

It is an accepted fact that bureaucracy can destroy initiative.

SOMEONE ONCE SAID:

Bureaucracy expands to keep up with the needs of an expanding bureaucracy.
—Isaac Asimov

As a leader in the organization, one of your responsibilities is to examine the various processes and their operational directives. Are they all necessary? Do they increase or hamper efficiency? Are they just make-work procedures? What is their effect on the morale of your people? Do they contribute to the accomplishment of goals and objectives?

CHANGE

SOMEONE ONCE SAID:

The future ain't what it used to be.
—Yogi Berra

The principal point made in **James Belasco's** *Teaching the Elephant to Dance* is that currently the most important function of a leader is the anticipating, planning, and implementation of change. He warns that the expression "We've always done it that way" spells doom for the organization if followed.

SOMEONE ONCE SAID:

The world has entered an era of the most profound and challenging change in human history.
—Stephen R. Covey

Change is a certainty. It can be beneficial or harmful. But it will happen, either brought about from within or from outside the organization.

SOMEONE ONCE SAID:

The measure of intelligence is the ability to change
—Albert Einstein

Spencer Johnson, in his best-selling book *Who Moved My Cheese*, clearly reinforced the idea that change is inevitable and that it should be anticipated, monitored, and adopted. Further, he said that individuals react to it differently. Some see it coming and make necessary adjustments and plans to implement it. Others, once they realize that change has come about, accept and embrace it and use it to their advantage.

There are some, however, who have difficulty with change. They might not actively resist it, but rather they ignore it and blindly go about life seemingly unaware that things are different. They continue to perform life's functions as they always have, getting more out of touch with reality every day.

Then there are those who realize that change is taking or has taken place, and they simply refuse to accept it and actively resist it. They believe that what is here and now is the ultimate, and it should not be altered.

The sad truth is that these latter types are bound for difficulties and failure.

SOMEONE ONCE SAID:

The secret of change is to focus all of your energy, not on fighting the old, but on building the new.
—*Socrates*

In this time of continual and often unexpected and unexplainable change, this is certainly true. Particularly if a "sacred cow" is involved.

> *ONCE UPON A TIME,*
> there was a police executive, actually the department head, who illustrated both of the negatives involving change. First ignoring its need and then actively resisting it.
> Several years ago the administration's human resources department, which controlled the personnel issues of the law enforcement agency, determined that

the time had come to overturn the department's practice of employing men only. This was publicly and stren-
uously opposed by the department head. He cited the
need for police officers to have above-average physical prowess, particularly strength and coordination.
And they had to have the ability to drive and shoot. His
department was at the time driving big sedans, and he
felt that many females would not be able to see over the
dashboard and would have difficulty backing one up
safely. Also, because of their small size, they would not
be able to handle a shotgun.

He believed that police work required the emotional
stability to handle violent situations and exposure to
extreme trauma. Further, he felt that most male officers
possessed these qualities and abilities and doubted
that females did. Simply put, females were not fit to do
the job.

When it was pointed out to him that several police
agencies were currently employing female officers,
he countered that yes, he was aware of this, but he
believed that for the most part the female officers were
serving as dispatchers and matrons, not real cops. And
he argued that most women would probably not want
the job, as the changing shifts and odd hours would
interfere with childcare.

The human resources representative cited several
studies that proved the opposite, and the department
head was directed by his superiors to amend his policy
and to begin hiring female officers.

The agency did so, although reluctantly, and within a
year had several women working on the streets. By every
measure, they were performing at the same level as their
male counterparts.

However, the department head was still resistant. He
often criticized their performance and discreetly warned
male officers to be wary of them and not to depend on
them for backup.

> It didn't take long for several sexual harassment and unequal treatment issues to develop and become public. Evidence against the agency head was substantial, he was forced to retire, and the jurisdiction had to pay a few substantial settlements.
>
> The agency head's career was over, and the department's image was severely damaged. And the change was made.

Even though a somewhat dated example, it illustrates both the initial ignorance of the need for change and once becoming aware of it, resisting and not accepting it. The executive failed to realize that hiring standards were changing and that law enforcement was no longer a strictly male domain. Rather than looking to see how his department could best accommodate and benefit from the change, he chose to initially ignore and then actually resist a nationwide cultural movement. This was much to his and the department's detriment. One can but wonder how he would have reacted to the LGBTQ movement.

Perhaps we can excuse somewhat this executive's views if he was instructed in management theories by former Chicago Police Department superintendent O. W Wilson, who publicly claimed that "manliness" is one of the qualities that employee oral boards should look for when evaluating police officer candidates. We know now that he was wrong.

SOMEONE ONCE SAID:

What used to be "nice to do" is now "must do."
—Tom Peters

Not only do we need to accept and deal with change from the outside environment, but we should be implementing change within our organization. Tom Peters advises that we should be soliciting suggestions and ideas from our employees and should be testing their validity. Perhaps initially you don't make a department-wide change, but in a trial mode, you can implement change on a lesser scale and measure results and acceptance.

Internal change can come about for a number of reasons. Modernization and technological improvements in the industry occur constantly in the communications, forensics, and record-keeping areas, and your department must keep abreast of them. And of course, there may be simply a better or more efficient way of doing things.

It appears to be human nature to resist change. This belief was examined by a communications scientist, **Everett Rogers**. In his book *Diffusion of Innovations*, he sought to explain at what rate new ideas were spread and accepted. His findings were that in any group of employees, about 15 percent are what he called early adopters. They are flexible and willing to try something new. In the middle group are the skeptics. They really don't care one way or the other. They don't particularly welcome the change but can take it or leave it. Fortunately, they make up most of your workforce, or 70 percent.

The final 15 percent are the actual resisters. They do not readily accept change and do so only if forced to.

This latter group of employees require an entirely different type of approach regarding an intended change. They need to be convinced of the necessity and the value of change to them and the organization.

Rogers recommended five steps to take:

1. Communicate the need for the change. Hold informational meetings, even one on one, to explain the reasoning and vision behind the effort.
2. Describe intended positive results and negative consequences for not implementing the change. If results are not going to be achieved immediately, explain why.
3. Make sure the employees have the knowledge and skills to implement the change and resultant job requirements, once it is implemented.
4. Develop an action plan that specifies roles and timelines. Build in a mechanism to obtain status reports to make sure the initiative is on track.

5. Have an after-action report that details the actual value of the change. And be sure to reward those whose efforts made success possible.

This appears to be a substantial expenditure of effort to convince a few, but if the change is necessary, it is generally worth it.

Change is the law of life.
And those who look only to the past
or present are certain to miss the future.
—*John F. Kennedy*

SOCIETAL AND CULTURAL CHANGE

As has been discussed, things are changing, not only on the job but society-wide, and there are few options on how you deal with these changes. Many see no need to make any adjustments. Again, the common "we have always done it this way" belief. Realistically, even though the old way might be working, as pointed out previously, with or without our approval or involvement, change is amending our practices and the world we live in.

SOMEONE ONCE SAID:

Every generation trash-talks younger generations. Baby boomers labeled Generation X a group of tattooed slackers and materialists. Generation Xers have branded millennials as iPhone-addicted brats.
—Neil Blumenthal

Just the passage of time has given us different cultural beliefs, and you will be dealing with several cultures.

First in line are termed the Baby Boomers, those born after the Second World War up until 1965. For the most part, those who are still working are not interested in change and sometimes have difficulty with it. They are not computer friendly. They are interested in retirement and maintaining friendships with their peers. They follow direction and for the most part are not a supervision problem.

After the Boomers are the Generation Xers. Born Between 1965 and 1985, they are generally more interested in the welfare of their grown children and aging parents than their jobs. Most have reached their employment goals and value their free time for pursuing personal interests and travel.

Next are the Millennials, whose birth and early years surround the turn of the century. They are eager for professional accomplishment, high pay and benefits, and opportunity and will work hard to get them. Currently, this is the group that if led correctly will contribute greatly to the success of the organization. In your department many will be supervisors or managers.

Last in line is the group called Generation Z. Many of this generation will be in the beginning ranks of your department. Most will have a college degree, and many are focused on monetary issues. They are starting families, and their concerns are financial and learning their chosen profession. Their beliefs may appear more liberal than law enforcement is accustomed to. For them, marijuana is not a problem and the death penalty is archaic and should be abandoned.

In addition to the necessity of dealing with a multitude of different personalities when managing people, added to that is now the necessity of understanding and dealing with a workforce comprised of several different cultures. Not only must distinct personalities be identified and worked with, but separate beliefs and unique temperaments based on cultural dogmas must be understood and contended with as well.

The key is understanding them. By knowing what types of beliefs they hold and what interests and influences them, management can construct a system that will motivate and satisfy them. Once again, you must know your people.

In addition to internal cultural changes that are occurring, society at large is on the move culturally, perhaps not always to the good, but the move is there and must be accommodated.

Whether we approve or not, there is now nationwide acceptance of marijuana use, a practice that constituted derision and a felony just a short time ago. Jurisdictions are now going back and removing records of felony marijuana convictions from an individual's rap sheet. Several states are looking at legalizing hard drugs as well. The

Netherlands, Switzerland, and Denmark now permit possession and use of cocaine, heroin, and meth.

Some jurisdictions have gone through a long stage of criminal justice law reformation. This has included the downgrading of many nonviolent felonies to misdemeanors, resulting in the release of thousands of individuals serving time in state prisons. Currently, violators are sentenced to county jail rather than prison. Many other crimes, previously classed as misdemeanors, have been reduced to infractions, so that the penalty of imprisonment has been removed.

Also the requiring of cash bail for the release of arrestees is on its way out.

What do these cultural shifts have to do with police management might be the question.

As a law enforcement leader, you must anticipate and be prepared to adjust your operation to change what is happening or going to happen. Not to do so will certainly result in personal and organizational failure.

Additionally, you must educate your employees both officially and informally. Get them to the latest schools. Not just police schools. Take advantage of local college courses, and again, not just police courses. Look into the psychological, behavioral, humanistic, and philosophical curriculums and assign your middle managers to attend.

The attitude of the agency starts at the top. Remember your visibility. If you make a practice of negatively addressing every societal change, your employees will do the same, and correct or not, that becomes the department's attitude. But regardless of the department's attitude, change will occur, and most likely the department will be viewed as out of step, behind the times, and nonprogressive.

The societal change will in many instances necessitate change in your operations and methods of doing things. These can be minor or transformational. In either case, you must make sure that you and your department adjust to it. This will include policy alteration, not just physically rewriting the policy, but in many cases actually changing behavior.

It is not the strongest of the species that survive, nor the most intelligent, but the one most responsive to change.
—*Charles Darwin*

TECHNOLOGICAL CHANGE

Another area of change that we must keep up with is the technological changes that are occurring.

We have lived in the computer age for some time, and without question, computers make day-to-day living easier. There is very little human knowledge that cannot be researched or learned via the internet. Now there are personal communications systems that enable the acquisition and dissemination of information, pictures, and videos immediately via handheld personal devices. A small handheld iPhone is capable of outperforming your old desktop HP or Mac. Just as Google replaced Merriam-Webster's, Siri and Alexa are making Google obsolete. You no longer have to look something up; just ask one of the ladies.

Dispatching via the radio is another facet of police work that is quickly disappearing and being replaced by technology. Units are dispatched via computerized text messages. The 10-4 interchanges between the dispatcher and the officer have been eliminated. On a purely humanistic plane, this is sad as quite often the dispatcher could pass along that human element of worry or concern that she picked up from the caller to the responding officer, reminding him to use caution. A printed text message fails to do that.

Methods of directing 911 calls from the citizen caller to the closest patrol units are being tested in some jurisdictions. Drones are answering some calls.

Many departments now have automatic license plate readers, so that by merely pointing the device at a plate, the officer can retrieve owner information and stolen status.

Even traffic enforcement has become more impersonal. The days of "bumper" or "odom" clocks, airplanes, and even radar in measuring speed are gone. Lidar has taken over. No longer are traffic citations handwritten; they're printed out on a handheld computer. Cameras record motorist wrongdoing and a citation is mailed to the vehicle's owner. Once again human interaction between law enforcement and the public is missing.

Violators now appear in court with their version of what took place, fortified by their in-car and iPhone camera recordings. Officers appear virtually or via an emailed statement.

Add to these changes the emergence of driverless vehicles.

There is now deoxyribonucleic acid, better known as DNA, which has substantially increased the ability to solve crimes. It is an advancement that adds favorably to police objectives similar to the development and use of latent prints a century ago. And as the database expands, DNA's value will increase accordingly.

Agencies no longer have to wait for reports of gunshots from the public. Shot spotters report directly to units, giving the number and location of the firearm activity.

In summation, these technological changes are here, and more will be coming. How you deal with the negatives and take advantage of those that are positive is important!

SOMEONE ONCE SAID:

**Sometimes we can alter change,
sometimes change can alter us.**
—Author

IMPACT OF TECHNOLOGICAL CHANGE

SOMEONE ONCE SAID:

If we continue to develop our technology without wisdom or prudence, our servant may prove to be out executioner.
—*General Omar Bradley*

Probably the most instrumental technology change affecting the population and having the greatest impact is the ability to communicate via the social media network. This technological expansion has not only expanded society's ability to communicate, it has greatly increased an individual's ability to network as well. This enables one to expound on and disseminate thoughts, views, and opinions, regardless of legitimacy or accuracy. Using Facebook, Twitter, and other social media, people can broadcast not just to friends, family, or a select few but to a worldwide audience.

No longer do we just let our closest associates know "the haps." What we put on the internet can be published and made available to everyone and anyone.

And with this increased ability to overcommunicate, instead of closer bonding and increased understanding based on shared interests, there appears to be a commensurate increase in insensitivity and antagonism between diverse groups and individuals.

Much of what people write, read, and share is clearly nihilistic and prejudicial. And frequently, when the police are mentioned, comments are usually negative and critical in nature.

Currently, because of these uncontrolled communications systems and structures, it is vital that every employee be aware of the destructive power of misinformation. Extreme care must be taken to avoid prejudicial or even the appearance of prejudicial behavior while utilizing social media. Each employee must have an awareness of his or her vulnerability and culpability through misuse of these communication systems, particularly if the remarks are made with departmental equipment or on agency websites.

At present there is no way to establish the accuracy of information being spread to the masses. In many cases, the originator cannot be identified. Yet such widespread reports are often taken as fact and many times acted on prior to verification.

> ### ONCE UPON A TIME,
> in a fairly large city, a young man was murdered in an extremely gruesome way. He had been shot, and then his throat had been cut to the point of beheading.
>
> Because of the brutal nature of the slaying, a rumor on social media began to spread that this was an honor killing.
>
> According to the dialogue, in the East Indian region, the Muslim culture demands that in the case of a pregnancy of an unwed girl, suspected homosexuality, or adultery, the perpetrator has to be punished. The retribution is usually carried out by family members and often in a bizarre fashion, including stoning and decapitation. These forms of punishment are administered because an individual had dishonored the family. They are accepted as part of the culture and not regarded by many as criminal.
>
> As it happened, the victim was Pakistani and there was a large Pakistani population within the jurisdiction. Subsequently, it was also learned that the young man was gay.

This suspicion was immediately spread on social media throughout the community and later even discussed in the official media. As can be expected, much negativity was directed toward the Pakistani community. There was a small demonstration at the local mosque, which the police responded to.

Given these circumstances, the police department was queried on whether or not it was investigating the homicide as an honor killing since it was carried out in accepted Islamic fashion and was possibly based on the boy's homosexuality.

The department responded saying that its investigation would certainly include inquiry along those lines but that it was receiving little cooperation from the Pakistani community.

Within a couple of days, the actual murderer was turned in by a snitch and arrested. The crime was gang and drug related, having no relation to Islam or Pakistani tradition. It was just a matter of one group attempting to make an impression on its rivals. Nothing personal.

Instead of the police receiving positive credit for the quick resolution of the crime, the opposite was the case.

Racial and anti-Muslim charges were brought against the department by the Pakistani community.

The mayor directed the chief to make a public apology and the city settled a threatened civil case out of court.

In this incident, the police were guilty of what was condemned earlier—basing belief and action on hearsay being spread on a public communications link that, because of its seeming accuracy, was believed to be true.

Police and community relations are difficult enough, particularly when they involve less than positive interaction with diverse communities. Incidents such as the one described destroy any hope of mutual trust between the groups.

With the abundance of uncontrolled communications systems, it is vital that law enforcement be aware of the destructive power of misinformation. Extreme care must be taken to avoid prejudicial or even the appearance of prejudicial behavior.

SOMEONE ONCE SAID:

We all make mistakes, but social media can frame those mistakes and display them infinitely.
—Anonymous

Unfortunately, these vast improvements in technology are not limited to productive society. Criminals, too, enjoy the sophistication of modern technology and have become "hi-tec." And use of these ultramodern systems is not limited to white collar–type crimes. A basic lawbreaker will own an iPhone and use it in ID thefts, drug deals, and online thefts. They can own a "burner" phone for less than $10. Most full-time crooks consider these phones disposable and have several.

Even while incarcerated, crooks have access to cell phones that are smuggled in to them. As an example of the power of this type of communication, it was discovered that the West Coast leader of the Sureños, a street gang, was serving a ten to life in prison, but that didn't interfere with his running the gang via cell phone.

TRANSFORMATIONAL CHANGE

SOMEONE ONCE SAID:

Transformation is a process, and as life happens there are tons of ups and downs. It is a journey of discovery—there are moments on mountaintops and moments in deep valleys of despair.
—*Rick Warren*

Up until now we have been discussing change caused by happenings outside the agency and the necessity and the means of responding to them. But an internal situation may arise that exposes the continued and prolonged neglect or mismanagement that the entire agency needs to change. Instead of simply observing what is occurring and attempting to make change to address and adapt to a situation, you may discover that the policies and procedures of the whole department are dysfunctional and out of step with the world.

Transformational change is where leaders work with their team to identify what major changes are necessary to improve operations. Together they determine what needs to be done and then work collaboratively to execute it. The involvement factor is motivational and increases positive morale. By being a part of the transformation of the agency, the participants take ownership of the results.

ONCE UPON A TIME,
a newly elected sheriff, coming from an outside agency, quickly observed that the day-to-day operation of the department he now led was sadly out of date and was in no shape to handle any kind of a crisis. It appeared to be struggling with simple routine operations.

In this instance, the cause was not simply neglect, but the department's profoundly old-fashioned practices and procedures. The outgoing sheriff had been in office for more than twenty years and, before being elected, had risen through the ranks, having nearly forty years in the department. The agency was functioning in approximately the same manner as when he first joined.

Some updates had been made as a matter of necessity. First-generation computers were in use, only because typewriters were no longer available. They were of the pre-mouse era and operated pretty much like an electric typewriter. The radio system had also been updated through necessity; otherwise, interagency communications would have been impossible. Radios in the patrol vehicles were, however, aged and undependable.

Equipment issued to the deputies as well for their training and day-to-day operations was also miserably outdated. Some deputies still carried revolvers and leather saps.

Department management was also behind the times. None of the policy manuals, directives, or general organization philosophies had been updated in what appeared to be decades. One general order still required that all "clamshell" holsters be inspected annually by a supervisor. Another cautioned against putting your foot on the violator's running board during a traffic stop, lest you upset the driver. What to do? wondered the new sheriff.

In their book *The Transformational Leader*, modern management authorities **Noel M. Tichy** and **Mary Anne Devanna** laid out solutions for just such an organizational situation. They studied just such problems and their solutions in companies such as General Motors, Chrysler, Honeywell, Burger King, and Chase Manhattan Bank. In each of these organizations they observed how the leaders came to grips with the need for change and how the process of transformation was implemented and accomplished. The blueprint for this process was outlined in three steps:

1. Recognizing the need for revitalization
2. Creating a new vision
3. Institutionalizing change

In their research, Tichy and Devanna noted that to make a successful transformation, all three steps had to be addressed. Also, an enlightened leader had to be involved.

Once it is recognized that a complete operational (transitional) change is necessary, employees must be convinced of that necessity. This is why formalizing a vision is absolutely necessary. Following that, implementing the change must be accomplished. Sometimes this can be quickly completed; in some cases, it may take several years or even a generation.

During the last half of the last century, American automobile manufacturers were faced with the increased popularity of imported Japanese cars. Japan had just recently entered the car business. The country had developed and utilized modern manufacturing methods and processes, such as replacing metal with plastic wherever possible in its vehicles. This simplified the construction, reduced costs, and provided operational savings because of the weight reduction.

It was a rude awakening for the American manufacturers that had produced their standard models and used the same construction methodology since the 1920s. Thus far they had been unbelievably successful and had seen little need to change.

SOMEONE ONCE SAID:

If it ain't broken, don't try to fix it.
—Bert Lance

Realizing that it had become unresponsive to consumer demands, General Motors Company implemented a large-scale operational reorganization affecting some 100,000 employees. In so doing the company had to struggle against years of bureaucratic management practices.

To implement the needed changes, GM created a transformational management team. This team spent more than a year in identifying what needed to be done and planning how to do it. One method the team used in overcoming reluctance of some was to institute participative management throughout GM. The team also introduced some innovative new products such as small- and mid-size models. The transformational process took more than four years before GM had returned to a competitive place in the world market.

Chrysler's transformation and recovery were accomplished under the guidance of Lee Iacocca, who because of his great success became a folk hero of the automobile industry.

Upon his initial taking over at Chrysler, Iacocca quickly realized that the management group didn't even realize that the company was in trouble. The group believed that its financial situation was normal and just part of the periodic swings in the automobile marketplace.

After realizing that Chrysler was broke and pretty much non-competitive with GM and Ford, in addition to the Japanese, Iacocca formed a team of managers whose sole purpose was to identify needed change and determine how to make that change. And they did so.

The managers developed a vision that included decentralization and a dramatic reduction in the workforce and at the same time increased quality and productivity from the remaining employees. They established networks of investors, managers, unions, suppliers, and dealers who believed in the vision and worked to make it succeed.

All three companies had utilized the transformational change process to remain functional in the industry.

Currently, because of the advent of electric, hybrid, and even driverless cars, the automakers are once again facing the necessity for transformational change.

ONCE UPON A TIME, CONTINUED

The new sheriff was convinced that change in the overall operation of the department was necessary, but there were those who were satisfied with the status quo, having the human nature to resist change. The sheriff realized that this resistance had to be overcome if revitalization was to take place.

In a unique way, the sheriff was able to convince most of the department's managers and employees who desired stability about the need for change and overcoming tradition.

Having some knowledge of the progressive qualities of several nearby sheriffs' departments, and with the agreement of those sheriffs, he assigned each of the employees on his management team to visit one of those departments. They were to spend one workweek at that department to observe and evaluate its operations.

Patrol, investigations, communications, the jail, and administrative functions were to be examined, as were policies and equipment being used. A report was to be made on each. The study was to be broad and all inclusive.

Upon their return, employees shared the reports and discussed them with the entire group. It was obvious to all that their department was deficient in most respects. The managers were impressed with the way other departments were conducting business and realized that it was advantageous and necessary for their department to follow suit.

The sheriff had accomplished the initial steps in the transformational formula by making it clear that change was needed and gaining agreement on that point. By involving management in identifying what similar agencies were doing and incorporating those practices in planned changes for the department, he had established management's support and acceptance of what needed to be done.

He next prepared and sent a survey to the rank and file requesting that they list any operational changes that they felt should be made. He was surprised at the number and quality of the improvements they proposed.

The next step was to create a vision. This was accomplished by further review of the reports and management's recommendations, plus those of the other employees.

Most employees were now cognizant that change was needed and aware of what had been suggested. And they could visualize the improved working conditions and overall benefits that would result from implementing what was recommended.

The final step in the process of executing the changes was at this point fairly simple. Acceptance by the majority of the employees had been achieved. The necessary training, budget issues, prioritizing, and planning the timing of the changes were the only tasks remaining.

Much like constructing a house, the foundation of each element of rebuilding the organization was systematically accomplished. Planned changes were initiated, and then built upon, until the updating of the organizational structure and its operations was completed.

The department would soon be in the twenty-first century!

Making a necessary "transformational" or major change in an organization is possible, but it is not a simple task. By following a process similar to that identified by Tichy and Devanna, it can be done. In some cases, it must be done

SOMEONE ONCE SAID:

**Transformational leaders create change
and leave legacies.**
—Farshad Asl

CRISIS MANAGEMENT

As you read and study how the various experts instruct how important it is for an agency to conduct formal planning and how it should be carried out, you will probably not come across a section on how to plan for or manage a crisis. Neither Fayol nor Odiorne mentioned it in their detailed planning instructions.

But it is important that you at least have an awareness of a possible crisis and give some forethought to your responsibilities in one. At the very least you should develop a basic idea of how to handle one.

Unfortunately, when members of the public become upset with the government, it is usually the police that they come into contact with, particularly if they choose to violently express their dissatisfaction. This usually will result in some level of crisis.

You will no doubt be faced with some sort of a crisis during your tenure.

The kinds of crises you will encounter may be of the natural disaster type: fires, floods, hurricanes, tornados, or even earthquakes. If you have lived in the area, you should have some idea of what has happened and what the law enforcement's response was.

The types of crises more specific to your agency's responsibilities are civil disorders, demonstrations, riots, multiple-deaths, or even terrorist activities.

The terrorist concern is national and political, and it's an area that law enforcement doesn't really want to be involved in, but they are. Terrorist acts, now classified as hate crimes, are occurring with greater frequency worldwide and throughout the United States. Formerly only of national concern, terrorism has created valid worry that has descended to the state and local levels.

Terrorist attacks are generally lone shooting or bombing incidents, but they can be substantially more. And although rare, they must be prepared for.

They are usually committed by a crazed US citizen who supports one of the recognized terrorist groups, such as the Islamic State in Iran and Syria (ISSIS), the Taliban, or Al Qaeda. And even more locally Antifa and the Proud Boys.

For incidents of this type, some sort of emergency response plan should be in place. Make sure to check that a plan is there and is up to date. If not, get busy on one. It is essential that emergency response plans are coordinated with a federal response.

In addition, determine whether these plans are coordinated with other agencies, not only first responders but others that might be involved postcrisis. These include hospitals, power companies, road departments, public housing authorities, and so on. It is imperative that they know what your agency is going to do and that you know what they are going to do. This should eliminate overlap and voids.

It is a good idea to get a buy-in from your local politicians for they will be heavily involved in a major incident. There is a possibility that you may need equipment replacement or additional funding. It is better if they have some idea of what is going on and can be ready to assist if necessary.

In the unlikely event that there are no civil disorder, terrorist, or disaster plans for your jurisdiction, start today in correcting this oversight.

The International Association of Chiefs of Police (IACP) some time ago conducted a series of seminars designed to gather information on the prevention and controlling of civil disturbances. Some of their teachings may be of some assistance to you.

The IACP advises the following:

- If they haven't already done so, agencies should work in tandem to develop up-to-date response plans that specify the roles and responsibilities of each participating agency.
- These plans should contain policies regarding the use of force, mechanics of arrest and containment, and general crowd control.
- Intensive training should be provided to all personnel who will be engaged in riot or disturbance control. This should involve cross-training so that participants know what the others are doing.
- Emergency communications systems between involved agencies should be constructed and tested frequently.
- Communication channels, if not in place, should be made with minority or other militant groups that might engage in civil disorder.

Again, these preparations are not just "nice-to-do things." They are measures that are essential to providing at least an adequate response to this type of a crisis.

SOMEONE ONCE SAID:

**A prudent person foresees the danger ahead
and takes precautions.**
—Proverbs 27:12

Know that your agency's actions and handling of the event will be closely scrutinized and evaluated at the conclusion of incident, so it is essential that you are prepared!

SOMEONE ONCE SAID:

By failing to prepare, you are preparing to fail.
—Benjamin Franklin

INTERNAL CRISIS CONTROL

Then, there is still another type of crisis, the internal crisis that you must be ready for. These crises involve your own personnel. Most of them are all too commonplace, involving alcohol, family, monetary, and other personnel problems that come with the territory. They are handled through the normal discipline procedure.

You may also be faced with off–duty or even on-duty criminal behavior, and once the justice system is through with its case, you can institute normal discipline. Sometimes, though, it is necessary to take disciplinary action prior to the judicial system. This is particularly true in serious crimes. If the departmental member is clearly guilty, job termination should be immediate.

The crisis aspect in any of these situations is normally not the act itself but the reactions to them created by the media and the public. Oftentimes there will also be a strong reaction from members of your own department or the police union if they disagree with your handling of the situation.

Any incident in which there is a suspected racial, ethnicity, or religious element involved, no matter how seemingly insignificant, can be cause for a crisis requiring scrutiny of the entire department, its policies, past behaviors, and preferential arrest statistics.

Some crises are of the scandal variety, which if handled incorrectly can result in the loss of public trust and possibly the loss of your job.

Other than your usual disciplinary policies, you may not have any written plans for handling scandals, but you should still be aware that if they become public, in spite of mitigation attempts, some negativity toward the department will result.

SOMEONE ONCE SAID:

The secret of crisis management is not good vs bad, it's preventing the bad from getting worse.
—Andy Gilman

The magnification of these seemingly routine incidents often happens without management having a clue, until they break wide open.

Involvement in these occurrences is not limited to lower-ranking personnel. Quite often agency leaders are involved. Crimes including theft, possession and use of narcotics, missing evidence, overtime scams, kickbacks, and felony sexual misconduct have been in the news.

Some of these misdeeds were committed by a member of executive management serving very close to the department head. In these instances, not only was the wrongdoing damaging to the agency, it was compounded by the question "Why wasn't the agency head aware of it?" Further, "Is the agency head involved?" And even more catastrophic, occasionally cover-ups were attempted.

These problems will usually come to your attention after an arrest by or information from another investigating agency, from an audit, or from a charged accomplice trying to lessen his penalty by making a deal. In the worst-case scenario, the media will request an interview and surprise you.

Remember, once discovered, action must be taken. Don't ever rely on a secret being kept.

SOMEONE ONCE SAID:

Three may keep a secret, if two of them are dead.
—Benjamin Franklin

So, what to do? There really isn't a good answer, but some type of action must be taken to maintain public trust and agency integrity.

ONCE UPON A TIME,
there was a chief of a medium-size agency who had been there for a number of years. Both he and the department enjoyed a decent reputation within the community. The chief was fortunate to have a second in command who had gone up through the ranks with him. There appeared to be complete trust between the two, and it was widely accepted that the assistant chief would take over upon the chief's retirement.

Even though the assistant chief's children were grown and gone, he maintained an interest in youth activities, particularly Little League Baseball. For more than a dozen years he had coached a team of eight- to ten-year-olds. Parents were extremely complimentary of his strict but patient treatment of the children. And the children worshiped him.

Then it happened. A fifteen-year-old boy was arrested for shoplifting. It was his second offense, which at that time was considered a felony if convicted. Even though a juvenile violation, it was not the type of thing one would want on his record.

The boy disclosed to his attorney that he had been molested in the past by the assistant chief in the hope that some kind of a deal could be made.

The attorney then went to the chief and told him of the accusation. The chief asked that some secrecy be maintained until he had time to look into the allegation.

Within two days, a reporter from a local TV station requested an interview with the chief to discuss the matter before the station broadcast it.

Because the assistant chief had been out of the area at training, the chief had not yet had the opportunity to question him about the allegation. He did, however, defend and express complete confidence in the assistant chief, explaining that the allegation was no doubt just a ploy by the juvenile to get out of the arrest. He went on to describe his long acquaintance and work history with his assistant. Further, he requested that the station hold off on a broadcast, explaining that unless the accusation was proven false, its airing would damage the assistant chief's and the department's reputation. The reporter said that she would try, but it was management's decision.

Once confronted, the assistant chief denied the accusation, relying on his many years of service and his unimpeachable record as a public servant and model citizen.

The following day the television news carried the story not identifying the boy but including a statement from his attorney.

The adamant denials from the chief and his accused assistant were also broadcast. There was no mention of a further investigation, giving the impression that as far as the department was concerned, the matter was closed.

After the initial news broadcast, three other boys came forward with stories of molestation by the assistant chief while playing on his little league team. One took place more than five years previous, the others more recently. The boys all claimed that they feared that if they had reported it, the assistant chief, given his position, would surely have arrested them for something. He had even implied that.

The secret was out! The community was in an uproar! Not just for the horrendous crime, but for the suspicion that had not the other boys come forward, the chief would have buried the complaint. It was even rumored that possibly the chief knew about it all along and was covering for his buddy. Questions were asked about what else was going on in the department that was also being covered up.

Public perception of the department declined as did morale within the department.

Facing prosecution, the assistant chief resigned. The chief was forced into an early retirement. Reportedly, to break up the "clique," he was replaced by an individual from the outside.

An internal crisis you will be faced with will no doubt be different from the above, but the quandary of what to do will be the same.

Sometimes the cover-up is worse than the crime. The truth stands.
—Anas Aremeyaw Anas

No matter how far-fetched the allegations may be, you cannot ignore them and you must immediately begin damage control.

The first thing to do is to try to verify the validity of the claims. Even if they are untrue, you must still take action.

Next, bring in your leadership team, brief them, and jointly decide on a strategy.

If your department has a public affairs officer, make sure that he or she is involved in these discussions, for the officer will certainly be questioned by the media.

Determine what the official response is going to be, and who will issue it and how.

When dealing with the media, know that delaying tactics with statements such as "We are still looking into the situation and will issue a formal statement later" won't fly and often do more harm than good. The media will quickly assume your strategy is a delay tactic and print or broadcast its own beliefs.

If I speak, I am condemned!
If I stay silent, I am damned!
—Jean Valjean

Be as candid and truthful as possible with respect to privacy and prosecution disclosures. If you purposely omit or fabricate and it is later discovered, the repercussions will be great.

Your message must clearly state that you do not and will not tolerate this type of behavior, that you are taking all possible steps to ascertain the truth, and that if wrongdoing did occur, you will assure that the perpetrator will be punished. Further, you should also state that you are taking steps to minimize any reoccurrence.

Be sure to brief your local politicians; hopefully, they will publicly support you and the department. It is also important to keep all department members up to date, as they, too, will be subjected to questioning by the public.

If a prolonged investigation is called for, consider asking an outside agency to perform it.

If your relationship with the public has been satisfactory, and your integrity has not been previously breached, you and the department will probably survive.

SOMEONE ONCE SAID:

The truth is incontrovertible, malice may attack it, ignorance may deride it, but in the end, there it is.
—*Winston Churchill*

Your correct handling of a potentially disastrous situation such as this will do far more to improve police and community relations than a career's worth of coffees with cops or other "officer-friendly" programs.

Again, complete honesty and transparency are the only viable responses that can be considered.

SOMEONE ONCE SAID:

Our greatest glory is not in never falling, but in rising every time we fall.
—*Confucius*

MORALE

Morale is an "iffy" thing. If your agency has high morale, you never even think about it; you just go on operating day to day. But then one day you may notice that things are not going too well interpersonal-wise.

A common indicator may be that the troops appear unhappy and are not giving it their all. Or if it appears that management seems upset for unknown reasons and to be questioning your decisions or direction, perhaps you have a morale problem.

The chief of one agency became aware of a morale problem when cartoons making fun of management were placed throughout headquarters.

Now, social media provides an even better avenue for broadcasting discontent.

SOMEONE ONCE SAID:

In war, morale conditions make up three-quarters of the game, the balance of manpower makes up the remaining quarter.
—*Napoleon Bonaparte*

In *Principles of Management*, Harold Koontz and Cyril O'Donnell agreed with Napoleon, advising that achieving and maintaining good morale is essential to the success of an organization. They loosely defined morale as "a prevailing spirit conducive to willing and dependable service including wholehearted cooperation and enthusiasm in performance of duty."

The measurement of morale is difficult, but if it is absent, as noted, observable general unhappiness results. Also, there does appear to be a high correlation between morale and productivity. If the workers aren't happy, they don't work as hard, and they don't give that little extra.

If you suspect poor morale, you must do something about it, and the first thing you must do is to try to figure out why.

The Human Resources Research Organization (HumRRO) is a nonprofit research organization that has completed studies for the US Army and numerous public and private groups believed to have morale issues.

HumRRO begins its inquiry with a survey designed to determine employee satisfaction or the lack thereof. The survey is then followed by corrective measures directed at the findings.

You are probably not in a position to conduct a formal survey, but listed below are the most encountered problems discovered in HumRRO's work, written by **Thomas Owen Jacobs** and published in *Leadership and Exchange in Formal Organizations*:

- Units with low morale did not have "employee-oriented" supervisors.
- In organizations where a leader did not take charge and lead, the result was "group instability," where employees felt tension and alienation toward the boss and one another.
- Antagonism toward excessive control systems that allow little employee discretion or flexibility in doing the job.
- Belief that management's production expectations are insatiable. No matter how hard employees try or how much they do, it's not enough.

Other common areas of discontent are inadequate pay and poor equipment. Correction of these deficiencies is not entirely in your purview, but they are important and must be addressed.

Unfair treatment either real or imagined can also lower morale. Management's perceived unresponsiveness to employee concerns is another area that can generate dissatisfaction. An overly aggressive punitive system caused a police strike in a major city a few years ago.

There is no need to conduct a formal study to determine whether a moral problem exists, but you can complete an assessment just by asking a few questions and taking a good look at your organization.

So far we have looked at how the experts have instructed us on how to motivate, recognize, and reward our employees so as to accomplish our goals. By following this humanistic approach to management, you will have a highly effective organization, and morale will not be a problem.

SOMEONE ONCE SAID:

**The best morale exists
when you never hear the word.**
—*General Dwight D. Eisenhower*

EFFICIENCY AND TIME MANAGEMENT

If you haven't done so by now, it is important that you develop good work habits. Efficiency is one of these.

Time is your most valuable resource. Sound time management is the key to getting things done.

In his book *The 7 Habits of Highly Effective People,* **Stephen R. Covey** listed time management as the third habit, or as he called it, "the principle of personal management." Covey encouraged organizing and executing around priorities, basically identifying areas of strategic importance and putting first things first. He believed that having the ability to do this consistently is the common denominator that all successful people share.

Covey identified what he termed "four generations" in the area of time management:

- Making notes and establishing checklists. This is an initial step in sorting out the requests and mandates on leaders.
- Utilizing calendars and appointment books. This is an attempt to look ahead and schedule future activities.

- Determining the relative value of activities and prioritizing actions.
- Focusing on enhancing relationships and accomplishing results.

His view was that this practice, which focuses on identifying and examining required activities and then rating them according to their importance and urgency, is the essence of correct time use.

Some matters are urgent but not that important. Others may be important but not urgent. Others may not fall in either category but still need to be done.

Effective time management then is identifying those items that are both important and urgent and addressing them first. The catch is having the ability to identify and properly classify the various activities you are faced with.

SOMEONE ONCE SAID:

Either you run the day, or the day runs you.
—Jim Rohn

To be an effective leader, Covey advises that concentration on the important items is the best course to follow. This course allows you to take a long-range view of the operation and concentrate on problem solving. The time spent on these efforts will provide improved and longer-lasting results.

Spending your time on nonimportant matters and continually responding in a crisis mode to seemingly urgent but unimportant matters is inefficient and nonproductive. Not only is it a waste of time, but those observing you will note your response to insignificant matters. When something really important does come along, they may write it off as just another noncrisis that the boss is responding to and not provide needed assistance.

SOMEONE ONCE SAID:

Lost time is never found again.
—Benjamin Franklin

Around the turn of the last century another business theorist, **Harrington Emerson**, studied efficiency and, like Frederick Taylor, believed that time was valuable and how employees spent it was important. Recognized as one of America's pioneers in management and organizational theory, Emerson developed basic principles of "management efficiency" and its importance to the organization.

In his classic book *The Twelve Principles of Efficiency*:

> **He said:** "The organization must have clearly defined ideals and know what its goals are, what it stands for, and its relationship with society."

Once again, take a look at the established purpose statement of your department. Is it current, precise, and meaningful? Does it accurately reflect your believed objectives and goals of the organization?

> **He said:** "The organization must have common sense and be practical in its methods and outlook."

This is basic. Make sure that you are attempting practical and doable tasks in a rational manner.

> **He said:** "The organization should seek wise advice, turning to external experts if it lacks the necessary staff expertise."

If you see deficiencies, those involving lack of knowledge or expertise, take advantage of available training opportunities. Take a look at what other agencies are doing; it is not unlawful to copy success.

> **He said:** "There should not be so much top-down discipline as internal discipline and self-discipline, with workers willingly conforming."

You should have obtained proper disciplinary knowledge and skills as you moved up through the ranks. Assure yourself that those below you are using the proper methods. If your management methods are correct, self-discipline should follow.

> **He said:** "Workers should be treated fairly at all times."

Again, simply use the management skills that enabled you to reach this level of command, and make sure that your subordinate supervisors and managers are doing the same.

He said: "All standards should be recorded in the form of written instructions, which detail not only the standards themselves, but the methods of compliance."

Check out your written policies and review and update them as necessary. This should be a scheduled activity, one carried out at least annually.

Emerson's principles certainly provide clear and practical directives for department leaders. Even though conceived in the early 1900s, they still have value today. If followed even generally, they should have a positive impact on your organization.

SOMEONE ONCE SAID:

The speed of the boss is the speed of the team.
—Lee Iacocca

Whether correct or not, slowpokiness is often interpreted as laziness. When people observe an individual habitually taking more time to complete tasks that are believed to be normal or necessary, they get the impression that the worker is not taking the job as seriously as he should be.

The question being, is the person incompetent, inefficient, or just lazy?

Emerson's efficiency principles point out that although the correct use of time is important in the worker's job, it is even more so in your job as leader. Being efficient is important!

SOMEONE ONCE SAID:

**Management is efficiency in climbing
the ladder of success; leadership determines
whether the ladder is leaning against
the right wall.**
—Stephen R. Covey

But remember, efficiency doesn't always equate with speed. Sometimes completing a task too quickly, or jumping into a situation before all the facts are known and understood, can lead to mistakes and inefficiency.

SOMEONE ONCE SAID:

**There is often in the affairs of government,
more efficiency and wisdom in
non-action than in action.**
—John C. Calhoun

Conversely, problems can arise by *not* doing something for the sake of efficiency, when just a little awareness would insist that efficient or not, something has to be done.

ONCE UPON A TIME,
in an ethnically divided community, there was an officer-involved shooting: a citizen was shot and killed by the police. The victim happened to be an African American. The officer was Caucasian. Immediately questions arose on whether the shooting was justified or just further confirmation of the police's race-based prejudicial behavior.

For several days following the incident, members of the African American community staged protests, first at the sight of the shooting, then in a city park, and following that, on the street in front of the police station.

As time passed, whether or not the shooting was justified became a forgotten issue. The sentiment of the protest became just anti-police and Black Lives Matter.

The gatherings in front of the station turned violent. Several windows in the station were broken by thrown rocks, and during the efforts to control the situation, two officers were injured and several demonstrators were arrested.

As it turned out, what was initially a skirmish between the police and the minority group was intensified by a radical group of white supremacists. Although they were not wearing white hoods, they were particularly antiblack and pretty much against everything African Americans believed in or did. Although they claimed their purpose was to support the police, the righteousness of the shooting actually had nothing to do with their involvement.

A few days later, the victim's family planned a huge parade after his funeral. It would start at the church, and following the service, the group would walk with the hearse to the cemetery.

The police didn't know about the parade until the funeral ended and the crowd assembled for the walk.

Once law enforcement learned of the planned parade, the chief determined that the department was not going to be involved.

The year before, the city council had presented the chief with a resolution honoring him for his efficient management of the department. For the third year in a row, the department had come in under budget, saving a lot of money for the city. The chief was extremely proud of this recognition and intended to repeat his success.

He took the importance of efficiency to the extreme, having a framed quote from Peter Drucker hanging in his office that proclaimed:

"There is nothing quite so useless as doing with great efficiency something that should not be done at all."

"Sometimes it is better to just not be involved" was the chief's view. "It's also cheaper."

Sometimes, though, it is better to be involved.

The white supremacists were.

When the groups met at the cemetery a riot broke out, the quelling of which required mutual aid being requested after the situation became so violent that the local police, once they responded, could not handle it.

As a result, several people were injured and several more were arrested.

When later questioned on why the police seemingly ignored what should have been known to be a potential problem, the chief explained that to his knowledge, funerals tended to be peaceful and respectful. Besides, his department already had devoted enough resources to this situation and the police were in danger of exceeding their budgeted overtime.

"Why should the other citizens be shortchanged police protection while officers were inefficiently watching over a funeral procession? Besides, a police presence might have created a problem," he rationalized.

He had convinced himself.

This decision was made without knowledge of how large the crowd might be, or if the antiblack group would be present. The need for traffic control wasn't even considered, much less the requiring of a parade permit. The chief totally ignored the event for reasons of efficiency and economy.

The chief lost his job. The dismissal was not budget related.

Even though the shooting was later determined to be justified, for the following several years, on the anniversary of the victim's funeral, a demonstration was held in front of the police station.

SOMEONE ONCE SAID:

Never sacrifice effectiveness for efficiency.

—Author

LEADERSHIP-LEVEL MOTIVATION

Earlier, Maslow's hierarchy, McClelland's achievement needs, and Herzberg's job enrichment approaches to motivation were discussed and recommended for consideration. They are all proven philosophies in the supervision and motivation of people and can be implemented individually or organizationally. Their previous suggested use was mainly for the individual supervisor or manager for the purpose of motivating their immediate subordinates.

What will be discussed here are motivational theories that can most beneficially be implemented at the leadership level for establishing a department-wide program.

In his book *GMP: The Greatest Management Principle in the World*, celebrated professor and author **Michael LeBoeuf** makes the argument that the very best way to motivate people is to reward them! He postulates that people respond to rewards, and if rewards are promised and delivered, employees will work hard to achieve them. He doesn't condemn other motivational theories, but he does claim that rewarding desired behavior for the purpose of motivating employees is the "greatest management principle."

He urges organization leaders to strategize and determine what they want to accomplish and then to develop an awards system to recognize and reward those who succeed in accomplishing the desired goals. This should not be a unilateral undertaking. Be sure to include your management team and also the labor unions or employee associations.

Call it what you will, incentives are what get people to work harder.
—*Nikita Khrushchev*

A reward-incentive program can be directed at individuals or units or can be organization-wide. Once this is determined, the next step is to identify meaningful rewards for the desired accomplishments.

LeBoeuf claims that organizations that offer monetary rewards for good performance get good performance! Unfortunately, financial incentives are not available for most governmental agencies. But there may be exceptions to consider:

- Some departments offer a shift differential pay scale. Normally, this is done to offset the undesirability of late shifts. Instead, suppose an identified police problem existed on a particular shift. The opportunity to work and continue working on that particular shift was geared to the individual's efforts and success in addressing the problem rather than to the time of day.
- Some departments offer skill pay for assignment as motorcycle or flight officers or expert investigators. In most, however, once an individual is assigned to the specialized unit, the pay goes on with little attention paid to performance. Continued motivation could be accomplished by establishing performance goals for these units, and only high achievers would be assigned and remain assigned.
- Longevity pay could be switched to performance pay. Longevity could be rewarded by giving additional vacation hours to senior officers rather than extra pay.
- Take-home cars could be offered as a reward for top performers.

Additionally, there are numerous nonfinancial rewards available:

- Hold an annual awards banquet where certificates or plaques are publicly presented to high achievers.

- Recognize an employee or unit of the month and afford them special privileges during the month. Perhaps use of specially designated parking places at the station.
- Offer promotions or special assignments.
- Give special accouterments for the uniform, pins, or patches.
- Prepare letters of commendation to be placed in employees' personnel files.

Positive feedback and praise are easy to bestow, and in spite of what Michael LeBoeuf wrote, many believe them to be more powerful incentives than money.

It is important that you be specific and sincere and personalize your praise for the specific accomplishment. By doing so you will avoid the impression of glad-handing, and it will be more meaningful for the receiving individual.

DELEGATION

Once you have your team built, it is time to look at their responsibilities versus yours. Time and its correct use are critical elements in successful leadership. It will not take you long to discover that you simply don't have enough time to do everything that you want to or are required to do.

SOMEONE ONCE SAID:

Be able to delegate, because there are some things that you can't just do by yourself.
—*Meghan Markle*

To delegate you should:

- Start by making a list of the tasks that you are expected to perform and those that you are performing.
- Next determine which are actually necessary. Eliminate those that are not.
- Determine whether there are additional tasks that should be completed.
- Also if you can, decide if some of the items remaining on the list could be better accomplished by someone else.
- Identify individuals who could perform the tasks and delegate the responsibility of performing the tasks to them.

In his book *Administrative Action,* **William H. Newman** explained that delegation is just determining who in the organization's hierarchy, other than the one in command, decides what and how things are to be done. And to effectively delegate at the executive level, a strong personal relationship must exist between the leader and the immediate subordinates.

This is necessary as these assistants exercise an amount of freedom and initiative in day-to-day operational decision making. And their decisions carry the same weight and importance as those made by the agency head.

As time and experience occur, lines will be drawn and either formally or informally limits of discretion will be arrived at. Actually, this is a practice that occurs at every level of command. Once supervisors and managers determine the interests and capabilities of their subordinates, they are often given the authority to decide.

The art of delegation, if it can be called that, is difficult and has some obstacles:

- You must first lose the fear of losing control and being overly concerned of outcomes. You must trust your people.
- Oftentimes the "boss" will succumb to an "I can do it better" belief. This may be the case, but in the interest of efficiency, if the subordinate is capable, let her do it. It contributes to the job enrichment theory and prepares her for advancement.
- To delegate effectively, you must be able to clearly describe the reasons and desired results of actions to be taken. It is then left up to the delegatee to determine the how-tos.
- There must complete confidence in the ability of the person delegated, or else there will be a reluctance to really let loose of the reins and overcontrol will result. And this will not result in lessening your time commitment or involvement.

SOMEONE ONCE SAID:

When you delegate tasks, you create followers. When you delegate authority, you create leaders.
—Craig Groeschel

Of equal concern when considering delegation is that not all subordinates welcome it. From their perspective it involves extra work, added responsibility, and risk.

Considerations when delegating:

- Some may view the getting of additional power and responsibilities as just inheriting junk jobs or busy work that the boss doesn't want to do.
- Sometimes it is necessary to delegate work that is not of a high priority to make time for more important matters, but this should be the exception rather than the rule. Always attempt to make delegated responsibilities meaningful.
- Along with the additional responsibilities, particularly where decision making is a factor, come the possibility and increased risk of making mistakes. Most people attempt to avoid risks.
- This is a valid concern, and as such, it is your responsibility to make sure the individual has adequate knowledge to be successful most of the time. If an error is made, it should be viewed as a lesson learned rather than a cause for criticism.
- Sometimes additional responsibility is not welcomed because the employee already has more work to do than can be accomplished properly through normal operations. In this case, the additional workload is not appreciated and is possibly even resented.
- Care must be taken so that the tasks to be delegated do not overburden the employee and that the taking on of additional responsibilities can be a positive and career-rewarding experience.

You may not encounter any of these difficulties in attempting to delegate. But should you, the steps you can take to overcome them are to provide encouragement, emphasize the positives, criticize carefully, and be there for necessary assistance. And as noted, establish and maintain as close a personal relationship as possible with your team.

Also, remember that delegation is actually giving direction and it is important how you confer it. As discussed earlier, direction given in the form of a question normally works better than a direct order.

A "How would you like to?" or "Can you do this for me?" will go a long way in gaining cooperation and acceptance.

SOMEONE ONCE SAID:

Don't tell people how to do things, tell what needs to be done, and let them surprise you with the results.
—General George S. Patton

INTEGRITY, CHARACTER, AND TRUST

SOMEONE ONCE SAID:

Leadership is a potent combination of strategy and character. But if you must be without one, be without strategy.
—*General Norman Schwarzkopf*

Almost every respected management authority lists integrity, character, and maturity as requisite qualities for a leader. In his book *On Becoming a Leader*, **Warren Bennis** advised that integrity is the basis of trust, and it cannot be acquired but must be earned and bestowed by fellow workers. They have to believe in you and further believe that what you say and do is morally the right thing. They won't get this belief by listening to you but by observing you.

John C. Maxwell, another leadership guru and respected author, lists integrity as a bedrock principle in his book *Winning with People*. Agreeing with Bennis, he considers trust as a major interpersonal requirement that cannot be possessed without integrity. He maintains that the moral honesty must be with yourself as well as with others. If you are not honest with yourself, it is impossible to be honest with others. Complete honesty brings about trust, resulting in integrity.

Merriam-Webster's defines integrity as "a firm adherence to a code of especially moral values; incorruptibility."

SOMEONE ONCE SAID:

It is true that integrity alone won't make you a leader, but without integrity you will never be one.
—Zig Ziglar

It should need no explaining why trust, character, and integrity are necessary for a leader or why they are necessary for an organization.

If a leader is to be that, a real leader, he or she has to have followers. If an individual is engaged in actions that for the most part are judged to be wrong by others, respect evaporates and confidence will disappear. So will followers. People, particularly in the police field, don't like to and won't work for a dishonest boss.

As leader of the organization you must set high standards. In his book *Character and Cops*, **Edwin Delattre** addressed the need for law enforcement professionals to set and abide by higher standards than the general public and other government officials. Even though this having more integrity than the others can be viewed as a double standard, it is an acceptable and necessary one.

SOMEONE ONCE SAID:

Character is doing the right thing when nobody is looking.
—J. C. Watts

Character includes your attitude, temperament, disposition, personality, ethos, and perhaps another dozen qualities. Your character is you, and it is on display daily, constantly.

You have a greater responsibility toward that general public—that of providing safety and security. If a police executive loses the trust of the people and cannot fulfill those obligations, the entire society suffers.

SOMEONE ONCE SAID:

Character matters; leadership descends from character.

—Rush Limbaugh

For any organization to succeed, there must be mutual trust between the leader and the followers, and between them, they then must create an organization worthy of the public's trust.

Unfortunately, there are law enforcement organizations that through their lack of or perceived lack of integrity have lost the trust of the people they serve.

ONCE UPON A TIME,
in a smaller community, a police captain went to a local pawnshop to look for a gift for his wife. He was shown a number of rings that were removed from the display case. While he was examining them, the shop owner was called away to the phone. Upon his return, the captain told him that the rings weren't what he was looking for and he left the store. When returning the rings to the case, the owner thought that one might be missing. He had installed a hidden camera that recorded activity at the display case. The video clearly showed the captain placing a ring in his uniform pocket.

The owner, acquainted with the chief of police, gave him a call and in confidence relayed his suspicion about the missing ring. He did not mention the evidentiary video.

The chief told him that he was most likely mistaken but that he would look into it. The next week, the owner once again contacted the chief. The chief assured him that he had spoken to the captain and that the owner was mistaken because the captain said he had returned all of the rings.

Knowing that his store pawned merchandise and was frequently subjected to police inspection and fearing retribution, the shop owner decided to not officially pursue the case. As far as the police department knew, the matter was history.

It was not. The shop owner was well known and respected in the community, and he "in confidence" spread the story, offering to show the video to doubters. Word spread quickly throughout the business community. And although the story remained only semipublic, the captain was privately castigated, as was the chief for his seeming indifference. As a result, an unspoken distrust soon spread to the entire department. Although no mention of the specific act was made, the local paper included an editorial of the rumored growing dissatisfaction with the police department.

Soon city leaders made changes in the police department's administration.

The shop owner still has the videotape.

In any group of human beings there will always be those who for various reasons do not always do the right things. Sometimes these are mistakes in judgment or, on the other end of the behavioral scale, outright criminality.

One doesn't like to believe it, but occasionally corruption exists at the top of the organization. There have been, and possibly are, police administrators actually involved in corrupt behavior. Or in other cases, administrators who just tend to ignore the situation or won't believe it is happening within their agency. Sometimes they may take steps to correct it but then attempt to mislead the public as to its occurrence.

Actions of this type illustrate a lack of character and integrity and certainly erase the trust of the public and employees.

SOMEONE ONCE SAID:

There is no higher value in our society than integrity.
—*Arlen Specter*

But why would police administrators, having reached the pinnacle in their chosen profession and having fought wrongdoing throughout their career, do wrong or even unlawful things?

If you have studied the Old Testament, you probably recall the story of King David seeing Bathsheba bathing and lusting after her. He ordered her brought to him and then sent her husband to a battlefield so that he would be killed. David married the widowed Bathsheba, but their first child died as punishment from God for his adultery and planned murder of Uriah, Bathsheba's husband.

King David's actions in this story have become known as the "Bathsheba Syndrome," or the ethical and moral failure of those in leadership positions.

Several years ago, a couple of university professors, **Dean C. Ludwig** and **Clinton O. Longenecker**, both management specialists, combined to propose a theory in "The Bathsheba Syndrome: The Ethical Failure of Successful Leaders." It was their belief that many ethical violations committed by lead executives were the byproducts of their success.

They believed the Bathsheba Syndrome to be valid based on the following:

- Success allows a person to become complacent and to lose focus, diverting attention from leadership to unrelated things.
- Personal success leads to privilege.
- With success comes unrestrained access and utilization of the organization's resources.
- Success can inflate an individual's ability to manipulate outcomes.

They profess that the combination of these dynamics can tempt even the most moral leader to believe that opportunities should be taken advantage of whether they are correct or not. The psychological impact of having power over others and the tendency for individuals and groups to overlook the wrongdoing of seemingly important people are given as the reasons for this. Simply said, power corrupts.

Studies have been conducted that show that leaders are in fact not held to a higher standard than others but to a lower one. Leaders were quite often granted lenience in terms of behavior and allowed to deviate from principles others must heed. The belief is that because they are so highly esteemed, leaders deserve a break if they do wrong.

History is replete with instances of those in leadership roles committing unethical acts. This includes politicians, coaches, priests, law enforcement leaders, and even several presidents. Thus an actual behavioral double standard is created. And similar to what occurs in the criminal area, not getting caught or punished if you do encourages increased misbehavior.

The authors conclude that organizations must examine and change structures that permit or encourage management to fall victim to the Bathsheba Syndrome. They recommend that leaders should lead a balanced life. Leaders also should build an ethical team around them, a team that is not afraid to point out lapses in correct behavior. This team should have a concern for the leader's personal-psychological balance and attempt to keep the leader on target.

SOMEONE ONCE SAID:

Success without honor is worse than fraud.
—Anonymous

Just having an awareness that the danger of straying exits and is real will hopefully keep most of you from straying off the path of integrity and good character.

Assuming that none of you are or will ever be engaged in malfeasance, the fact remains that sometime in your career as an executive, you may encounter serious wrongdoing by an immediate and trusted subordinate. If so, unlike the chief in the "Once upon a time" tale above, it is critical that you respond to it correctly.

No matter how removed or insulated you believe you are, and how perfect and professional your behavior has been, there will always be some negative attachment to you and certainly your agency if anyone at a high level is involved in a transgression serious enough to attract media attention.

Therefore, at the first inkling or suspicion of any wrongdoing it is imperative that you initiate damage control.

SOMEONE ONCE SAID:

Honesty is the best policy.
—Sir Edwin Sandys

The best way to do this is to initiate a full disclosure, staying within privacy regulations and protecting prosecution as necessary.

There will still be negativity, but as was learned from a presidential incident in the 70's, attempts to cover up the act often result in worse repercussions than does the act itself. Being forthright from the start will do much to salvage public trust both in you and in your agency. Forthrightness also illustrates integrity.

SOMEONE ONCE SAID:

The cover-up is always worse than the crime.
—Andrew Hall

HUMILITY

SOMEONE ONCE SAID:

humility: the quality or state of being humble
—Merriam-Webster's Collegiate Dictionary

The experts that we have studied have enumerated all of the recommended qualities that leaders must possess and the manner in which they should project those qualities. You must have strength, knowledge, courage, integrity, vision, and so on. However, one virtue in particular is rarely mentioned.

In his *Agma* (sacred works), **Gautama Buddha**, the fifth-century religious leader and founder of Buddhism, instructed:

> It is hard indeed to feel humble, to know respect and honor, to get rid of all attachments, to keep pure in thought and deed and to become wise.

Yes, it is hard, but you must strive to do it.

In learning how to instruct, correct, give direction, and delegate, Buddha instructs us to use tact and suggestion rather than the straight exercise of power that the position you hold gives you. The correct belief is that your subordinates will more readily comply with your wishes if you give them in a more humane manner.

By now, your basic approach to leadership has been formed. If it doesn't contain a degree of humility, it's an area that needs improving. You do not need to reinforce your position and power repeatedly.

The less people speak of their greatness, the more we think of it.
—Francis Bacon

Many leaders view a certain amount of arrogance as a necessary symbol of power. It just comes with the territory and perhaps is an element contributing to success. If that supposition is true, it follows then that many leaders believe that they are inherently better in some way than the people they lead. Actually superior in most ways. If this is your belief, you might want to consider changing it.

Lorin Woolfe makes a strong argument for a humble approach in his book *Leadership Secrets from the Bible*. He uses Moses as an example.

Moses is considered as truly one of the most successful and powerful leaders of all time because of the many things of note he accomplished. He bested the Pharaoh to free his people, and he parted the Red Sea and received the Ten Commandments from on high. After accomplishing all of this, he had every right to be a haughty and conceited leader. Instead, he became clearly the opposite.

Moses was a very humble man, more humble than anyone.
—Numbers 12:3

According to the Old Testament, at various times Moses would fall face down and protest that he was not worthy to lead. Yet lead he did, giving us all a lesson in humility.

Demonstrating the trait of complete honesty by accepting blame for your mistakes is one way **James Belasco** in his book *Teaching the Elephant to Dance* proposes humility as a primary trait for leaders. With their enormous size and power, elephants could dominate the bush, yet they choose to be harmonious rather than dominate. They are large, possessing great strength, but choose to be humble and nonaggressive unless challenged. Belasco urges leaders to be the same and to leave their egos at the door. Success depends on the cooperation of everyone, not a continued display of power by the person in charge.

Nobody likes to make mistakes. They are even less desirable for a leader to make, because as you climb higher in the organization your mistakes become more obvious to others and affect a greater number of people. This all too often causes leaders committing even small errors to sometimes deny the slipups or even blame others. This failure to admit error is often more problematic than owning up to a mistake and correcting it.

Being humble enough to admit it when you are wrong often increases your strength as a leader, for people react positively to displays of humility rather than to an attitude of being too big to make or admit to mistakes.

SOMEONE ONCE SAID:

**Humility is not thinking less of yourself,
it's thinking of yourself less.**
—C. S. Lewis

In this business as well as in life, we all play different roles and have different responsibilities. Some may be important and have actual or perceived status, while others may not, but we are all human and important in our own right.

ONCE UPON A TIME,
a sheriff of a medium-size county who was coming up for election was beginning to receive public criticism for his department wasting time and spending excessively in order to control the illegal growing of marijuana. Many citizens believed that legalization rather than continued criminalization should be the approach taken. But at the time, dealings with the drug were state felonies and a federal offense. Plus, he considered marijuana to be a gateway drug and that society was better off without it.

The sheriff learned that the negative attention regarding the pot program was being brought on by a sergeant in another agency who was planning to run against him in the upcoming election.

According to the sergeant, marijuana control was a wasteful and unwise effort, since marijuana was not that big of a deal and was someday going to be legalized. His campaign mantra was "Let's catch murderers, not farmers".

The sheriff was well aware that marijuana was being grown in agricultural areas of the county, sometimes with the permission of or even by the landowners. He also knew that international drug cartels sponsored the larger gardens.

In attempting to control what he viewed as a major criminal enterprise, he had created a special drug enforcement unit within the investigations division, which during the growing season concentrated all its efforts in trying to locate the grows and eradicate them.

It soon came to the sheriff's attention that the sergeant's campaign was in large part being financed by one of the farmers on whose land his drug unit had discovered a large amount of marijuana being grown. The invesigators believed that the owner had knowledge of and was permitting the grow, but they were unable to prove this.

Concerned, the sheriff met privately with the sergeant and confided his concerns. In the meeting the sheriff was not threatening, but he explained that it would not be good for the sergeant's or law enforcement's reputation if shady politics were to be made public. He urged the sergeant to cut ties with the individual in question. He also assured the sergeant that this issue would not be made a part of the campaign on his part.

The sergeant was extremely thankful, immediately dropped out of the electoral race, and publicly rescinded his statements about marijuana growing.

The sergeant found it incomprehensible that someone as important as the sheriff would take the time to meet with him, a low-ranking individual who was not even a member of his department, particularly since he had vigorously attacked the sheriff's pot program. Plus, the information the sheriff possessed about his campaign financing could have ruined his reputation, not just in the sheriff's race but in his career in his own agency. For it was in fact the very landowner and contributor who had encouraged him to make antimarijuana enforcement the centerpiece of his campaign. The sergeant also believed the sheriff when he stated that he would not bring up the marijuana farmer's support issue during the election.

Some might believe that the sheriff's motive was to remove a competitor in the upcoming election. Actually, because there was still another candidate for the office, having the sergeant in the race was beneficial for the sheriff, as two candidates running against him would split the opposing votes.

As the sergeant realized, the sheriff didn't have to meet with him or warn him of the possible predicament he might be getting into through association with a suspected drug grower.

Without going into detail, the sergeant announced the reason for withdrawal from the sheriff's race was that the current sheriff was such a fine and humble public servant.

Remember, honesty and a little humility go a long way.

SOMEONE ONCE SAID:

Pride is concerned with who is right.
Humility is concerned with what is right.
—*Ezra Taft Benson*

SELF-DISCIPLINE

SOMEONE ONCE SAID:

You will never have a greater or lesser dominion than that over yourself. . . . he who cannot establish dominion over himself will have no dominion over others.
—Leonardo da Vinci

Successes and failures in your life and career up to this point have in large part determined how much self-discipline you possess and practice.

The importance of how you are and how you appear has been mentioned several times, but it is being brought up again because of its significance at the leadership level.

SOMEONE ONCE SAID:

When strict with oneself, one rarely fails.
—Confucius

In case you haven't noticed, you are continually on a stage with a huge audience. The public, the press, politicians, peers, and most importantly your subordinates continually view your actions and behaviors. And it is on these observations that judgments are made. And it is these judgments that often determine whether you win or lose as a leader or in life.

The observed actions are not always on a grand scale. Sometimes small behaviors can make a difference, such as inattentiveness at meetings, improper wearing of the uniform, or impoliteness by simply ignoring a greeting. These small actions may seem unimportant, but these are the types of things that are noticed. These are the types of things that you must pay attention to.

So what is self-discipline?

SOMEONE ONCE SAID:

Self-discipline is that which truly and essentially raises one man above another.
—Joseph Addison

As quoted previously, self-discipline is "doing the right thing when no one is looking." But it is more than that.

It's living what you preach and what you expect from others.
It's obeying all those seemingly insignificant rules and regulations.
It's obeying the law.
It's coming in early, working late, and taking work home with you.
It's putting in time on the weekends.
It's not kissing off "callouts" or delegating disagreeable tasks.
It's demonstrating honesty and integrity in everything you do, both on and off duty.
It's taking a personal interest in the members of your department.
It's being faithful to your friends and family.
It's not passing the buck but accepting blame when warranted.
It's being a true leader.

That's self-discipline!

SOMEONE ONCE SAID:

Most powerful is he who has himself in his own power.
—Seneca

CONTINUE WINNING

Again, congratulations to you for having reached the position of a high-ranking law enforcement officer. And having done that, it can be assumed that you are a winner. Whether through hard work, natural ability, or just plain luck, you have made it to or near the top of your chosen profession.

But now that you're there, you can't relax, although you may be tempted to do so. At a minimum you must continue to devote the same amount of interest, energy, and dedication that got you there. If you lead a smooth-running operation, you must keep it that way. If your agency hasn't peaked, you must get it there. You can accomplish this by trying to follow the advice of the experts we have so far discussed and continuing with the supervisory, management, and leadership practices and skills that have served you so far.

Nationally, the average period in office of a chief of police is three years. It's even shorter for some department heads.

Let's make your tenure longer.

SOMEONE ONCE SAID:

Whether you're having setbacks or not, the role of a leader is to display a winning attitude.
—General Colin Powell

Dr. Denis Waitley, in *The Winner'–s Edge*, makes the point that to continue winning, you must have an attitude of "cooperation" rather than "competition." What he is suggesting is that instead of viewing every problem as a battle, a win-or-lose situation, look at it as an opportunity to maybe have a win-win solution. This is particularly important if the problem involves differences of opinion.

The differences can be between yourself and your top managers, political bosses, the unions, and even the workers.

SOMEONE ONCE SAID:

Conflict cannot survive without your participation.
—Wayne Dyer

Always seek compromise.

Achieve this by thoroughly examining all sides of the problem and giving each equal consideration. This examination should include obtaining feedback from those groups mentioned above.

> *ONCE UPON A TIME,*
> a chief in a mid-size department was confronted with a problematic situation over which he seemingly had no control. His city had gone through an incorporation process in which it had gained jurisdiction over several sections of mostly undeveloped land. The area did, however, include the county fairgrounds.

Day to day, the fairgrounds did not cause problems for the department. Infrequent calls consisted mainly of alarms at some buildings and an occasional trespass. Additional patrol necessary during periodic auto races and an annual rodeo was mostly subsidized by the sponsors of these events and covered on overtime.

This situation changed substantially during the annual ten-day county fair. This event brought well-known entertainers, carnies, and thousands of attendees. Along with these came the expected police complications.

The chief was approached by the fair board wanting assurance that security would be provided. Board members explained that they had not budgeted for security as it had previously been provided by the county.

Down several officers due to injury leave and normal vacancies, the chief begged off providing full-time patrol service during the fair, offering instead to have the surrounding beat units patrol close to the fairgrounds for immediate response if necessary. Additionally, they would make periodic walk-throughs. Further, if a situation required it, perhaps the sheriff could assist.

The fair board and the city decided to supplement this arrangement by hiring a private security firm to provide a continuous-presence patrol both while the fair was open and at night.

This resolution for the most part was successful until two local street gangs attended the fair on the same evening and encountered one another.

Shots were fired, killing one participant and injuring two civilians. Both police and sheriff's deputies responded, but well after the fact.

As can be imagined, there was a tremendous outcry from the public and the media blaming the fair board, the city, and the department for the lack of security. Particularly the latter two. The county grand jury also issued a highly critical report on the lack of security at the annual fair.

SOMEONE ONCE SAID:

Change is vital, improvement is the logical form of change.
—*James Cash Penney*

The chief was told that change and improvement were necessary.

Initially, the chief met with his team, requesting its input. Team members all agreed that with existing resources, even by using schedule adjustments, canceling days off, and vacations during the fair period, proper patrol of the fair was impossible for the department to handle alone. Use of overtime was out of the question as just utilizing it for this event alone would almost wipe out the entire budgeted amount. He thanked the team and reluctantly agreed.

Next, the chief approached the sheriff. This resolution was not available either. The sheriff stated, "Sorry, when it was in the county, we did it. Now it's yours." Knowing that argument was useless, he thanked the sheriff for the assistance at the recent fair.

Next, the chief went to the city council requesting an overtime supplement. This, too, was refused. He thanked the council for providing the private security, not mentioning how ineffective it was.

Frustrated, the chief was ready to publicly proclaim that his department could not provide adequate protection during the fair. He was even ready to suggest that it be canceled if the city and the fair board could not provide funding for adequate patrol. Realizing that this would probably be a career-ending move, he didn't do it.

Instead, at an area law enforcement leaders meeting, he discussed the problem and his frustration with his peers. The suggestion was made that he start a "reserve" program. The department was currently engaged in a loosely organized "volunteer" program, and several of the volunteers could be elevated to a reserve officer

> level by providing the minimal required training to those qualified and interested. They could then be utilized in a low- or no-pay status and provide the protective patrol during the fair. The chief did so.
>
> By the time of next year's fair, there was a well-trained volunteer force of reserve officers to provide patrol and crowd control as necessary.

The chief in this example, even though receiving blame for the tragic events that occurred at the fair, did not respond negatively and try to shift the blame. He demonstrated Dr. Waitley's recommended principle of cooperation over competition.

He could have accused his underlings of poor management by not scheduling officers to patrol the fair. He could, as he contemplated doing, placed blame on the fair board and city officials for not providing sufficient resources. He chose not to do that either, instead initiating a search for a solution and providing one prior to the next year's fair.

This chief would continue to win.

SOMEONE ONCE SAID:

Yesterday's home runs don't win today's games.
—*Babe Ruth*

In his book *What Got You Here Won't Get You There*, **Marshall Goldsmith** explains that oftentimes the knowledge, skills, and attributes that assisted you in becoming a leader and winner may not be enough to keep you successful.

SOMEONE ONCE SAID:

To be or not to be, that is the question.
—*Hamlet*

For the most part your success was achieved through your own efforts. There may have been some guidance and advice that assisted you, but it was mainly you.

Goldsmith says that was great, but that was then. You must now take a look at ways to continue winning. He lists several negative habits that some winners have acquired and recommends that you check to see if you have perhaps added them to your behavior:

The habit of passing judgment on every issue. The opinion or information given you can be clearly wrong, but try to avoid immediate dismissal. Try remaining initially neutral on issues. Thank people for input and for giving you something to consider. You don't have to continually show your superiority by immediately knowing what is right. Also, sometimes you may be wrong.

The habit of making destructive comments. Even though you might agree with what someone is saying, don't always qualify your response with a "yes, but" or a "sure, however" and then go on to make your point. People may quit coming to you with proposals or suggestions if you continually have to verbally improve their thoughts and subtly put them down.

The habit of speaking when angry. If you are upset, the chances are that you might say something that you will later be sorry for. If you do this repeatedly, you may get a reputation for emotional volatility. People avoid angry people.

The habit of withholding information. It is said that knowledge is power, but not sharing information so that you are the only one in the know may give you temporary power but often at the cost of loyalty.

The habit of claiming credit that you don't deserve. You can be forgiven for not bestowing credit on deserving people, but you will not be forgiven for claiming credit for their achievement.

The habit of clinging to the past. That was then, this is now. People really don't appreciate being reminded of all your successes and how great you were and are.

Goldsmith's theory is that once you have achieved success, many of the problems you face are behavioral rather than technical. Specifically, the manner in which you interact with subordinates. If you acquire and display these negative and damaging habits, your winning ways may not continue.

SOMEONE ONCE SAID:

Our success does not turn on what others do to us, but on what we do ourselves.
—Frederick Douglass

A more positive look at maintaining the winner's edge is included in another volume. In their book *Credibility: How Leaders Gain and Lose It, Why People Demand It,* **James Kouzes** and **Barry Posner** detail the necessity of maintaining successful leadership in an organization through the development and use of "credibility."

They instruct that achieving credibility involves exercising "consistent honesty" with your employees. You do this by saying what you mean and meaning what you say and then doing what you say you will do.

SOMEONE ONCE SAID:

Relationships feed on credibility, honesty and consistency.
—Scott Borchetta

As you became a leader, others gained trust in your abilities. Now you must keep that trust. The authors outline six key areas that are involved in their thesis of "credibility," which they maintain is the key to continued winning leadership:

- You must clarify your values. This is done by being honest with yourself and with your employees. Followers want leaders who are honest. A corollary to honesty is consistency. Leaders are consistent and competent. All of these are values to adopt, and they all build confidence. Confidence in yourself and trust from your followers.

- Identify your people's needs. As acknowledged by Maslow, individuals have needs. Make the effort to communicate your understanding of those needs and attempt to accommodate and align them with departmental purpose. Everyone desires safety, security, recognition, and rewards with success to follow.
- Build consensus. Involve people in decision making. Stimulate their interest in and get their buy-in in the organization's goals and objectives. This should result in progress in that same direction.
- Communicate with enthusiasm and conviction. Be passionate in your dealings with your subordinates. Display your genuine interest in them, and your combined efforts and responsibilities will reap positive response and rewards.
- Stand up for your beliefs. Display confidence in your decisions and direction. This in turn will inspire confidence in you. At the same time don't be too rigid. Be open to input.
- Lead by example. Actions are more important than words. Again, credibility is gained by what you do rather than by what you say.

Kouzes and Posner's views on how to continue winning after you have successfully climbed to or near the top in your agency are certainly worth study and application.

SOMEONE ONCE SAID:

Do not follow where the path may lead. Go instead where there is no path and leave a trail.
—Ralph Waldo Emerson

As was recommended for middle managers, you, too, must continue to learn.

School is never out for leaders, so you must keep learning. Added to the knowledge we have gained from the experts we have studied thus far are a vast number of new and developing authorities inventing even more modern theories and concepts of supervision, management, and leadership. Keep leaning, listen to them, read what they have to say.

SOMEONE ONCE SAID:

The person who doesn't read is not ahead of the person who can't read.
—Dr. Sheila Bethel

Through life experience, your daily reading, or formal training, if you are exposed to inspiring or meaningful thoughts, you should record and remember them. Since you all carry an iPhone, an iPad, a laptop, or all three, you have on hand the means for doing so.

Once recorded, you can and should review them periodically. They are also handy when you are encountering a problem or uncertainty where some advice or special wisdom may be needed.

SOMEONE ONCE SAID:

The discipline of writing something down is the first step toward making it happen.
—Lee Iacocca

FINALLY

Now that you have been exposed to the teachings of the masters on how to become successful as a supervisor, manager, and leader, we will examine other topics.

SOMEONE ONCE SAID:

Success is not final; failure is not fatal: it is the courage to continue that counts.
—Winston Churchill

CONCERNS AND SUGGESTIONS

Up to this point, general principles associated with basic supervision, management, and executive leadership have been addressed. The how-tos. These doctrines have been studied and proven through use. Recognized experts have written of them and not only have endorsed them conceptually, but have operated under them. Both industry and government have successfully applied them, including many law enforcement leaders.

What follows is a slight deviation from these accepted theories. Simply reflections and thoughts based on personal observation and experience, they certainly do not hold the weight of the accepted and recommended practices of the experts but are offered solely in an advisory capacity.

POLITICS

SOMEONE ONCE SAID:

**Politics determines who has the power,
not who has the truth.**
—Paul Krugman

You probably realize it, but if not, as has been said, be aware that you are now in a highly visible and highly political position. This means that everything that you do, or fail to do, will be critically observed and judged, and not always fairly.

In your department there will be those whose support is undying. There will also be others who no matter what action you take on any issue will question it.

Your decisions and behavior will be under critical scrutiny. Not always in admiration, but sometimes for other reasons. This is an unfortunate circumstance, but a reality. Once at the top, you gather enemies as well as admirers, so it is prudent to watch your back.

SOMEONE ONCE SAID:

Et tu Brute?
—Julius Caesar

It may be for reasons of envy or jealousy. The cause may be revenge, if they believe that you treated them unfairly on your way up. Possibly they want you to fail so that they or someone they admire more can replace you.

In addition to these internal issues, there can potentially be some negative public opinions and pessimistic judgments arrived at and, valid or not, freely publicized.

Much of this you will have dealt with before, for unfortunately there are people who dislike law enforcement and everyone associated with it. You've met with them and dealt with them on the streets. And not all of your nonfans will be at the street level; some may be high in business or government.

Then there are others, seemingly your friends, who believe if they can advance their position or popularity by demeaning you, they will do it.

These criticisms may be inaccurate, unfair, and potentially career damaging. But they will happen.

Unless there is a direct attack on your honesty or morality, most of these assaults are better ignored. A high-powered response often brings increased attention and undue credibility to unimportant issues. You are not being urged to "forget and forgive," but unless these accusations are creating irreparable damage to you or your agency, deal with them judiciously and discreetly as possible.

SOMEONE ONCE SAID:

Half a truth is often a great lie.
—Benjamin Franklin

But if someone is truly impugning your virtue or integrity, you must dispute and correct it; ignoring it could cause irreparable damage to you and the department.

One of the first things to be done is to try to determine the source. Sometimes the rumors or allegations themselves will give you a clue as to their cause, basis, and origination. Once you discover the reasons for the animosity, you can most likely correct untruthful perceptions.

Discovering who is demeaning your character will give you the opportunity to make things right and take whatever corrective action you deem necessary.

Am I not destroying my enemies when I make friends of them?
—Abraham Lincoln

The real danger of politics is that it can sometimes have a disastrous impact on the agency's operation as well as on the people involved.

ONCE UPON A TIME,
the newly elected governor, as was custom, replaced the director of a state-level law enforcement agency. The ousted agency head had been in place for a number of years and was genuinely liked and respected by department members, and it had been hoped that no change would be made. Further irritation was garnered when the replacement came from "outside" the agency and did not possess an extensive or impressive law enforcement background.

"Pure politics" grumbled the department's executive management. Most, although not openly, determined to passively resist any changes the new director might want to make.

The new director sensed this attitude and, instead of trying to repair it, responded by assuming an arbitrary and almost tyrannical leadership style.

Almost immediately, a divisive issue arose. The new director had been directed to reduce departmental spending in the upcoming budget. After a few nonproductive attempts to involve executive management in finding a solution, the director made an independent decision to downsize the type of patrol vehicles in the departmental fleet. This downsizing included both the body style and the engine size. Thus, initial purchase and operational costs could be reduced.

After gaining approval for the purchase from the administration, the vehicles were obtained and put into use. Throughout the department, personnel in all ranks expressed extreme displeasure, with both the vehicles and the director. The complaints concerned safety, performance, and comfort with regard to the vehicles. Incompetence and lack of caring with regard to the director.

The union representing the officers and sergeants was particularly vocal. It published articles and appeared on TV complaining about this change coming from a director who they suspected had never even been in a patrol car.

Executive management did little if anything to defend the decision or the director.

As luck would have it, within three months after the new vehicles were deployed, one was involved in a horrific accident, and the officer driving it was killed. The investigation disclosed that the officer was at fault, having lost control while traveling at an extremely high and unsafe rate of speed.

The cause of the accident had virtually no impact on mitigating the outpouring of negativity, again toward the vehicle and its unsuitability for police patrol and the director who had foisted it on the department. Once again, the union led the charge, going to the governor, the state legislature, and the public demanding that the director be replaced for incompetence. Some even urged that he be held civilly liable. The officer's wife appeared on TV and repeated the union's demands.

Politics kicked in, the pressure became too great, and the director was replaced.

A retrospective examination of the actions of several executive-level managers he had inherited indicated that those individuals played a part in his undoing. They had never accepted him as the department head. With regard to the vehicle-downsizing decision, they now claimed that they had not supported it and had agreed with the criticisms about its suitability. Once the tragedy occurred, their attitude was "told you so."

The lesson to be learned: politics coupled with disloyalty can be your undoing. This includes both those you work for and those who work for you.

In addition to proving the absolute necessity of loyalty, this example provides proof of how change must be recognized as a critical event in an organization's existence and survival. Both the change of directors and vehicles should have been handled better.

SOMEONE ONCE SAID:

I used to say that politics was the second-oldest profession. I have come to know that it bears a gross similarity to the first.
—Ronald Reagan

Politicians may want to use you, your position, and your credibility to support their favorite causes or even their reelections. Be careful in doing so. This is often difficult as sometimes your appointment and the department's budget depend on their good favor. If you do so, do so only when you honestly believe that what you're doing or saying is the right thing to do.

And know that if you do not do as requested, be prepared to explain why, and live with possible repercussions.

NOTIFICATIONS

It is imperative that you have a policy that clearly dictates when you must be personally notified of events that are important to you and the department and that occur in or affect your jurisdiction.

This notification policy not only should be included in the department's general orders, but it also should be a part of special orders for various units such as dispatch and shift commanders and even down to the first-line supervisor's special instructions. And it is even more important that all supervisors as well as your dispatch or communications center must not only be aware of the directive but adhere to it.

This "notification requirement" should include natural or man-made disasters, that is, fires, earthquakes, floods, riots, events having multiple deaths, and incidents involving known personalities. In some agencies, even homicides are cause for notification. Some incidents may be of such a magnitude that even if they do not occur in or even adjacent to your agency's responsibilities, they may have some effect on your responsibilities and you should be aware of them.

Also to be included should be departmental occurrences: officer-involved shootings, officers injured or arrested, and so on. Any occurrence that has the potential to attract media attention should be included.

The list of reasons for and who is to be notified in any of these situations can be as extensive as you want it.

SOMEONE ONCE SAID:

**What you don't know, won't hurt you.
A dubious maxim: Sometimes what you don't
know can hurt you very much.**
—Margaret Atwood

The primary purpose for your being notified is obvious. You need to have firsthand knowledge of significant happenings in or near your jurisdiction. This knowledge affords you the opportunity to determine what, if any, action needs to be taken, and if action is being taken, is it the correct action? Additionally, there may be notifications that you must make.

Prompt notification allows you to assure that available resources are sufficient and, if not, to take corrective steps. Moreover, if it appears that you are unaware of what's going on, lack of confidence in your ability to lead may occur.

SOMEONE ONCE SAID:

**In order to make timely and correct decisions,
leaders have to know what's happening.**
—Author

Whether or not you respond to the scene is your call. In most cases, it is better to have gone than to later wish that you had.

Your response indicates to your people, the public, and the political entities over you that you are interested and involved.

It also provides you the opportunity to observe those doing the actual work and to gauge their effectiveness. Plus, it gives you the opportunity to immediately prevent or correct errors if necessary.

At times you may have to settle jurisdictional disputes with other responding agencies such as the fire department, coroners, and sometimes even the district attorney. Your being there will oftentimes eliminate the "who-is-in-charge" argument.

One caution, though: when you do respond and observe that everything is going well, stay out of it and let your people do their jobs. Ask if you can help and offer assistance if needed. But otherwise, just observe.

INCIDENTS WITH VIPS INVOLVED

One instance in which you probably would rather not be notified, but it is important that you are, is when some high-profile individual is caught breaking the law by one of your officers. Undesirable as these situations are, an occurrence of this type *must* be on your "notification" list.

Most of the time, after the circumstances are explained, the question posed is, should an arrest be made?

The individual involved is more often than not a politician, a celebrity of some sort, or maybe another cop.

In some cases, after all of the necessary evidence has been collected, you may decide to file a complaint at a later time rather than make an arrest. If you choose to handle it in this manner, stand by for criticism from the public, the media, the individual's political opponents, or anyone who has an issue with the person or his or her station in life, particularly if the complaint route is not the usual method of handling that particular type of circumstance.

Experience has shown that it usually works out better if an arrest is made.

SOMEONE ONCE SAID:

There is no VIP, we are all the same.
—Machine Gun Kelly (gangster, not rapper)

Once done, and you are assured of the validity, it might be beneficial for you to respond to the jail, ameliorate the situation by easing the booking process, and possibly keep the arrestee out of a cell or the drunk tank. Normally, once notified, an attorney can arrange some sort of release.

If it is an officer from another agency, protocol and common courtesy require that you notify that department head.

Another notification that should be made, if not done so already, is to your public affairs person. Once the information gets out, and it will, you must have a prepared and professional response as to what actions your department took, or didn't take, and why.

UNIFORMS

The New York City Police Department started wearing uniforms in 1854, and most agencies have adopted their use. The reasons are obvious: they identify the community's protectors, and the visible presence of law enforcement reduces crime. There have been numerous studies conducted on the psychological impact of uniforms on the public.

The experts state, and probably correctly so, that the clothing worn is very important in the initial development of social relationships. On the positive side, uniforms demonstrate power and authority and provide citizens with a sense of safety. The negatives expressed primarily by antipolice factions are that the uniforms portray a militaristic image indicating that the officers are at war with the citizens. And that they are worn as a means of intimidating the public.

This may have some validity. In the sixties when civil disturbances and antiwar riots were commonplace, some agencies made the wearing of helmets instead of hats part of the patrol uniform. Helmets are clearly identified as a military item worn during wartime.

Even today, because of the great amount of gear that officers must carry, some departments permit and may even require that outer vests be worn. These, too, tend to make the officers look more like combat soldiers than cops. This may contribute to the intimidation concerns some members of the public have.

As a result, a few years ago, some departments experimented with switching to softer uniforms. They put patrol officers in sport coats and slacks in order to promote their community policing programs. But when resisting-arrest incidents and assaults against their officers increased, they quickly reinstated the police uniform.

The great majority of law enforcement leaders today believe that the wearing of the uniform by officers is important. It is essential, not only for identification and the performance of their duties, but for the pride most of them feel in wearing it.

SOMEONE ONCE SAID:

**A policeman in plain clothes is a man,
in his uniform he is ten.**
—Mark Twain

True for the troops, but there is a difference in the wearing of the uniform by the department head.

If the reason you wear it is for ego or narcissistic reasons, you shouldn't. Sure, those stars on the collar look great, and you have worked hard for them, but oftentimes the wearing of a uniform will interfere with developing a cooperative relationship with some citizens. As stated previously, there is an intimidation factor, and some members of the public, whose favor you need, may be turned off by the officiousness a uniform portrays.

Just as some citizens are intimidated by your officers in uniform, so are many of the people whom you meet with—other government officials, community leaders, and even some politicians.

There are formal, official, and public occasions when the uniform should be worn, and there are occasions when it should not.

Avoid wearing it to social gatherings and never to a political function or a potentially embarrassing media encounter.

ONCE UPON A TIME,

in a fairly large city several officers were accused of assaulting a citizen and faced a highly publicized trial that ended in their acquittal. As the case had racial overtones, a huge number of people were unhappy with the verdict. This unhappiness resulted in major rioting throughout the city. Later, the police response was criticized as being inadequate. Critics determined that the chief was not available to take immediate command as he was engaged in personal business. This chief normally appeared at official functions and press briefings in full uniform, and he looked splendid in it. However, on this occasion, when subsequently interviewed by the press and questioned about his absence on the night the riots began, he appeared in a suit. His desire was to personally accept the blame and minimize the damage to the department. He did so by not presenting a visual image of a police officer. Well done!

The uniform is intended to present a sharp, neat, and fit appearance. It should display pride in your department and your profession. Therefore, it is imperative that when you do wear your uniform that it be immaculate. Most members of the public will not notice "gigs," but your staff certainly will. They will be your biggest critics, so you must look good. If you are noticeably overweight, please wear a nice suit instead.

PUBLIC AFFAIRS

One of the certainties in life for a law enforcement executive is that the media will be involved in some fashion in almost everything you or your agency does, especially now that almost everyone has the ability to record "live" what your officers are and are not doing.

It is rare that citizens or the media for that matter video your officers committing a heroic act or handling a tough situation correctly. But if a mistake is made, it will surely be recorded and viewed by the multitudes.

Transparency is the word of the day for all public agencies, particularly the police. No longer can or should an agency cover up or attempt to hide wrongdoing, however slight. And this is as it should be, for like it or not, the citizens are the boss and the media the watch dogs.

And the press certainly exercises this expressed freedom.

It therefore becomes obvious that unless national security is involved, or an investigation where release of certain information might jeopardize the prosecution or the individual's right to a fair trial, it is absolutely necessary to cooperate with the media.

One practice that should be avoided is to have the agency head identified as the sole spokesperson for the department. There are a couple of reasons for this.

Most important, if you misspeak, it hard to correct, as it is assumed that you know all of the facts, and if something you say is untrue, you lose a great amount of credibility. There might be the thought that you intentionally misspoke in order to deceive or, alternatively, that you just didn't know what you were talking about. If a spokesperson does so, it is more acceptable and forgivable. Save your statements for a formal press conference once all of facts are known.

Second, as the agency head, your exposure to the press should be limited to important items. Overexposure lessons the importance of the times when you actually have a need to speak for the department.

Many agency heads hire or appoint someone to be the spokesperson for the department. This person's job is to report on ongoing routine matters and be the media contact.

A public affairs person or officer is extremely important and a "must-have" position for your agency no matter its size.

Your activities are highly visible and of great public interest. Almost every activity or incident that your department is involved in will make the news, newsworthy or not. The media is going to report on every occurrence it hears of, and in most cases, it is better that the story come from the department rather than someone with an agenda.

in his book *Corporate Public Affairs,* **Otto Lerbinger**, a professor emeritus at Boston University specializing in applying social science to management, instructs that in an organization there are three operational levels: the executive level, where responsibility is lodged; the professional level, where knowledge resides; and the technical level, where skills predominate. A public affairs official, centered in the middle or professional level can serve as a counselor to the executives, as well as provide assistance to the technical level. Translated to a law enforcement agency, it would mean that public affairs should be conducted at the middle-management level, possibly by a lieutenant or captain. Not many police administrators would agree with this, believing that the management skills of an individual at that rank could be better utilized elsewhere.

A solution might be to have a nonuniformed public affairs person. Once trained, this person can handle the day-to-day press releases, live on- scene interviews, Facebook, Twitter, and other social media as well as a middle manager.

A non-sworn or civilian public affairs person may be desirable for a couple of reasons. First, if a story is less than positive, it is better for the media audience to see someone in civilian clothes describing, defending, or whatever than someone in a uniform. Save the police presence and image for the positive stories where the department looks good.

Additionally, the cost of a sworn officer is much greater than that of a civilian. And an officer is much more valuable to you, the department, and the public performing real police duties. Most taxpayers believe that if they are paying for protection and service from an officer, that officer should be doing that, not propagandizing.

Plus, by hiring a civilian, you may be able to get someone who has had training and experience in media affairs.

Again, to make an impact on the media and the public when needed, save yourself for the really meaningful occurrences.

SOMEONE ONCE SAID:

Public opinion is the thermometer a leader should constantly consult.
—Napoleon Bonaparte

Following is an example of what could be termed a paradigm shift. In this case, there was a department head who believed that he was a "darling of the media" and much loved for personally reaching out to the public in order to improve police citizen relationships, but it did not work out that way.

ONCE UPON A TIME,
there was a chief of a smaller department who apparently believed that the public's right to know was paramount and that it was his personal responsibility to assure that that right was fulfilled. Perhaps, though, it was his personal ego, and his personal reporting on the happenings in his agency's jurisdiction, that provided him with the means to fill that need.

In any case, no matter the relative importance of the occurrence, if his agency was involved, he would address the media at the scene or call a press conference. Or, at a minimum, personally dictate a media release to be distributed and hopefully reported on or published.

One could count on his being on the local news almost daily. If it was a routine burglary, with no remarkable features, he would pontificate on either the dramatic increase or the dramatic decrease, due to his department's diligence, in burglaries. Added to this would be a short sermon on how to protect your property.

This routine was relentlessly followed and included almost every activity the department was involved in. It was rumored that some exaggerations were made for the sake of adding drama and maintaining interest.

One newscaster solemnly warned the citizenry to avoid getting a parking ticket, lest they become notoriously exposed via the chief's crusade.

Claiming his perhaps sincere desire to improve police-public relations, he copied the "Coffee with a Cop" program, where citizens could meet with law enforcement in a local restaurant and express their concerns. Of course, the meetings were with him, not a cop, and of course the media was invited. Citizens could now have "Coffee with the Chief."

The chief's hubris was so apparent that the press and public alike began to suspect that he had some type of narcissistic affliction.

His next endeavor was a "Citizen's Police Academy," starring him. The media soon termed it the "Chief's Show," and it became a local joke. The academy was mostly attended by people not really interested in police operations, and it became more of a social gathering for retirees or a place to be seen.

Then one day, a female dispatcher filed a sexual harassment complaint against the chief. The lady was young, single, and quite good looking. She claimed that at the department's annual Christmas party, the chief had followed her into the restroom and attempted to kiss and fondle her. There were no witnesses. The chief denied it.

During the ensuing investigation, she took a lie detector test and the results were inconclusive. For unknown reasons, the chief did not consent to taking a polygraph. The complaint remained unresolved.

The dispatcher left the department. She did not seek any type of financial settlement. The mayor and the city council were displeased with the chief, believing he had brought disrespect and shame on the department and the city, and sought his resignation.

The chief, claiming innocence and based on his past unblemished record, appealed to the public to rally behind him. He was, he believed, popular and admired by the citizens of the city.

However, most likely owing to overexposure, the chief's credibility had suffered. Suffered to the point that the public no longer took him seriously. The result being, they did not get involved or provide any assistance or support. Letters to the editor in the local paper were condemning. And social media was harsh and unforgiving. He resigned shortly thereafter.

The moral to the story is: if you are the department head, public relations are a must, but let someone else do it day to day. Overexposure may lead to dislike and disrespect.

SOMEONE ONCE SAID:

Half the harm that is done in this world is due to people who want to feel important.
—T. S. Eliot

No matter how well intentioned, anything can be overdone.

COMMUNITY RELATIONS

After the extremely violent and hugely antipolice decade of the six-ties, law enforcement leaders sought ways to reduce the citizen-cop tensions. This gave birth to the "community policing" movement that was the recommended path for departments to take.

Beginning in the mid-seventies, the movement endeavored to portray the "officer-friendly" image, stressing that the police were here to help, not hurt. In the nineties, the federally endorsed pro-gram, Community Oriented Policing, or COPS program, was handed down to local agencies accompanied by federal funds.

Former law enforcement officer and ranking executive **Dr. Wayne L. Davis**, in his book *Police-Community Relations: Bridging the Gap*, provides guidance and insight in administering a community rela-tions program. He defines community relations as a philosophy that uses partnerships between the police and the public to proactively address problems such as crime, social disorder, and public safety in general. These programs serve not only to create a means to involve the public in the process of finding solutions but to improve the image of the police. If correctly planned and administered, commu-nity policing programs should be successful.

SOMEONE ONCE SAID:

I Believe in community policing. And, in fact violent crime is one-half of what it was. . .
—Hillary Clinton

Various forms of the effort consisted of holding periodic meetings with the public, sponsoring ride-a-longs, citizen academies, and forming neighborhood watch programs.

Claims were made of vast reductions in crime, but as pointed out previously, crime statistics are not a reliable source for measuring program results due to ever-changing population numbers and alterations in criminal laws.

SOMEONE ONCE SAID:

Community-based policing has now come to mean everything. It's a slogan. It has come to mean so many different things that people who endorse it, such as the Congress of the United States, do not know what they are talking about.
—James Q. Wilson

Although community policing was well intended, the elimination of animosity toward the police from some didn't occur. Good citizens like and support the police, bad people do not. Programs do little to alter this fact. Soon community policing joined the revolver in obsolescence.

The Officer Down Memorial Page, a nonprofit group in Fairfax, Virginia, that honors fallen police officers, reports that from 1990 to date there are an average of 164 officer deaths in the line of duty every year, most of which are violent in nature. This seems to indicate that adoption of the officer-friendly image hasn't helped much.

The number of citizens killed by officers annually has stayed about the same as well. Historically, the greatest impact on citizen deaths by officers had nothing to do with public relations programs; it was the US Supreme Court's 1985 *Tennessee v. Garner* decision, which held that "it is not better that all felony suspects die than that they escape." Consequently, most departments altered their shooting policies to restrict shooting an individual unless lives were in danger. And as result, fewer fleeing felons have been shot.

Given the above statistics, many police administrators are reevaluating the value of their community service programs, believing that perhaps the time and effort expended could be better utilized on actual crime-fighting functions.

Unfortunately, times again appear to be changing. Citizen groups akin to those that existed in the sixties are emerging. Their credo this time is that minorities are treated differently by the police than are whites, particularly when it comes to the use of deadly force. There are some movements by state and local governments to defund the police. Some entities are passing laws and ordinances that restrict law enforcement to respond to particular calls for service that involve mental disorders, homeless individuals, or drug offenses. Mental health specialists, drug counselors, human relations personnel, and even firefighters will be dispatched instead. It will be interesting to see what will result if these changes are made. Public relations may improve, but public safety will surely suffer.

Currently, however, your best goodwill ambassadors are your officers. They meet dozens of citizens each shift, and each contact gives them the opportunity to improve community-police relations.

OFFICER-INVOLVED SHOOTINGS

Other than being notified of the injury or the death of an officer, an officer-involved shooting is perhaps the next most unpleasant notification to receive. But unfortunately, these occurrences do happen.

In the past, the only real concern for police administrators regarding officer-involved shootings was officer safety. "Is our officer injured or worse?" was the initial and primary worry. Of lesser interest was the condition of the other involved parties.

Once the medical status of the involved officers was established and necessary treatments provided, for the most part, the investigation was handled similar to other shootings. Crime scene diagrams were made, statements taken, reports completed. The only additional task was the determination of whether the firing of the officer's shots was within policy.

This has changed dramatically. A shooting where an officer happens to kill an individual now merits national news. This is particularly true if the victim happens to be a minority. It makes little difference if the officer is also a minority. Unfortunately, when deadly force is used, it many times becomes a racial issue. And it also only slightly lessens these concerns if the shooting was completely justified.

It is unfortunate but true; many citizens, many members of the media, and many politicians view the police as borderline terrorists who repeatedly employ Gestapo-like tactics against the citizenry. To have an officer shoot someone simply reinforces those beliefs.

It was noted earlier that one of the first things that you should do as a new administrator is to review your agency's policies. One of the first policies that must be reviewed is the shooting policy.

You probably are aware that the policy cannot be based solely on statutory law. In one state, the law still justifies the killing of fleeing felons or felons resisting arrest. It was passed in 1892 and is still on the books. Needless to say, this statute has been superseded and guidance is now provided by case law, which has greatly restricted the use of force by officers. But even case law is being questioned by "liberal law," which believes that no matter the circumstances, police should not shoot people.

Thus, you had better be on your game if an officer-involved shooting takes place. And your officer-involved-shooting policy had better be good and adhered to.

SOMEONE ONCE SAID:

**Don't write so that you can be understood;
write so that you can't be misunderstood.**
—William H. Taft

After a thorough review of the shooting policy, needed revisions should be made. Try to avoid vagaries or inconsistencies, particularly in the "when-to-shoot" narrative. This is difficult when such terms as reasonably necessary, reasonable belief, and probable cause are contained in law.

The fact is that the legality of shooting has pretty much gotten down to: the officer's or someone else's life has to be in actual and articulable danger to justify the firing of a weapon. No longer just a reasonable belief or suspicion.

And to this point, in several states there have been moves to legislatively substitute "actual" for "reasonable" in the law.

Realistically and unfortunately, cell phones can be easily mistaken for weapons, and almost everybody has one in their hand or are reaching into their pocket for one. Officers are aware of this. And it is this type of human behavioral change that administrators must also know. And policy changes must follow!

The shooting policy should be a living document, under constant review and altered as necessary, not just words in an underused manual.

Once reviewed and updated, the policy should then be presented to the prosecuting attorney in your jurisdiction, and the question asked: If one of our officers is involved in a shooting, and it was done in a manner permitted by this policy, will you agree that it was lawful? It might even be a good idea to get that approval in writing.

Once you have a policy, it must be trained. It should be frequently reviewed at briefings and, on range day, be built into shoot, don't- shoot exercises.

Even if an officer-involved shooting may appear to be lawful and within the approved policy, that is helpful, but the battle is not over.

The department's findings can no longer be based on the officer and witness statements as most metropolitan areas now have surveillance cameras designed to record every incident that occurs 24/7. Plus, almost every citizen has a cell phone capable of recording anything occurring in sight. Add to this the fact that currently most police vehicles have dash cameras and many of the officers are wearing body-worn cams (BWCs).

When introduced, the vehicle and officer-worn cameras were intended to assist in gathering and recording evidence to support an arrest. Now, however, it seems that their purpose has shifted to document and substantiate police misdoing.

SOMEONE ONCE SAID:

In the era of angry and aggressive policing, it is an honorable service to your fellow citizens to video record police officers' interactions with the common people.
—*Steven Magee*

Just be cognizant that without fail, the details of the incident are well documented, if not by your agency or by a citizen, then by a camera protecting some commercial establishment.

Therefore, it is extremely important that the statements given and reports written by the involved officers be completely accurate. Members of the public might get excited about the shooting itself, but they become even more enraged if they perceive that the police are untruthful and perhaps attempting a cover-up.

SOMEONE ONCE SAID:

**I'm not against the police;
I'm just afraid of them.**
—Alfred Hitchcock

It is also extremely important that any statements given to the media be correct, for media outlets are looking for a big story, and something negative about a police shooting is a big story.

SOMEONE ONCE SAID:

**The truth is incontrovertible.
Malice may attack it, ignorance may deride it,
but in the end, there it is.**
—Winston Churchill

Most departments have a policy requiring the placing of the involved officer on what is termed administrative leave, until after the shooting investigation is completed.

This practice should be evaluated. Shooting someone is an extremely traumatic occurrence, particularly if a life is taken. Should the officer be isolated, away from companions who can provide emotional support at this critical stage?

ONCE UPON A TIME,
there was an officer-involved-shooting incident where the officer was killed. This occurred in the daytime in a residential area. When the officer originally came under fire, a "shots-fired" call was put out to officers on the adjacent beats. A short time later, when the first responding

officer arrived, the original officer was dying, and after a brief exchange of fire, the suspect fled while the second officer attempted first aid.

The assisting officer immediately blamed himself for the victim officer's death, as he had gotten lost in the housing tract during his response, adding a few minutes to his arrival time. He repeatedly berated himself, claiming that if he had gotten there on time, he could have helped and possibly saved his beat partner's life. It became immediately apparent to management that the officer was experiencing deep depression, a condition now termed posttraumatic stress disorder (PTSD).

As he had discharged his weapon at the fleeing suspect, in accordance with policy and practice, he was placed off duty on administrative leave until the shooting investigation was competed. And as was normally done, he was provided with psychological assistance. Apparently, the officer interpreted this action and the forced separation from his friends as a condemnation. A short time after returning to work, he committed suicide.

Most agencies have a protocol that automatically sends officers involved in particularly traumatic events to counseling. This service is provided by trained experts, who, though they are professional, do not know the officer and oftentimes do not fully understand what the officer might be facing.

There is normally some guilt, no matter how justified the shooting turns out to be. And in many cases, this determination may take weeks or months to be arrived at. Even if the result is positive, and the officer vindicated, a huge amount of stress has no doubt been built up.

Then, if it is in fact found to be an unwarranted act, the officer may be facing punitive action from the department, up to and including dismissal and, in extreme cases, criminal prosecution. All of these procedural and administrative dealings could be as traumatic for the officer as the actual shooting incident was.

Rather than exiling shooting-involved officers after the event, a better approach might be to temporally remove them from the field and place them in an administrative assignment. This would reinforce the feeling of belonging to the organization. Their being surrounded by supportive fellow department personnel is by far more therapeutic than the impression of isolation they receive when placed off duty and sent home. Plus, you can still send them to counseling and more closely observe their posttraumatic demeanor.

Recently, law enforcement critics have complained that when an officer shoots somebody, he or she gets a paid vacation. This is another reason to give it some thought before placing your officer on leave following an on-duty shooting.

SOMEONE ONCE SAID:

I get by with a little help from my friends.
—John Lennon

You or a member of your executive team must go to every officer-involved shooting. This is important, as it lets the officers and the public know of your interest and that you place high importance in these incidents.

DIVERSITY

Years ago, there was a fairly successful attempt to alter the makeup of law enforcement in both the ethnicity and gender categories. The move was called affirmative action. At the time, in order to achieve "balance" in agencies, preference in the testing process was given to the underrepresented classes of candidates. On the surface this seemed unfair, but for the agencies this was not problematic as long as hiring standards were maintained. As a result, police agencies became more balanced racially and gender-wise. And they are better for it.

More recently, though, the diversity concept has moved on. Race, gender, and ethnicity are no longer the sole traits of diversity. Additional factors have been included. Homosexuality may have been a concern for some, but it was never an actual problem. We now, however, have transgender individuals, whether through surgery or just by their beliefs, who are a reality and in the workforce. You will be facing these sexual orientation and gender identity issues. Some departments are currently encountering problems in locker room and restroom use and officer interpersonal relations. Whatever control measures you take must be justified, reasonable, and legal.

Another problem recently faced by a chief was that one officer's religion required the wearing of a turban. This definitely did not fit the department's uniform policy. The chief consulted with top management and met with the union, and a decision was reached to permit an exception. No doubt, the public noticed it, but it never became an issue. Had the department done otherwise, it may well have become a major one.

This twenty-first century is overloaded with diversity issues that will continually test your resilience and patience. One state recently passed a law requiring that the boards of directors of big corporations must have at least one female on that board. Failure to do so would result in a $100,000 fine. Surely it won't be long until this mandate will be expanded to apply to governmental agencies.

Also under consideration is the removal of the citizenship requirement for law enforcement officers. It is believed that this would be a great way for immigrants to become assimilated into America. And if the population makeup of the jurisdiction is the same as the non-citizen officer's nationality, it could be beneficial, as he or she could better identify and communicate with a minority community. Their continued employment would be contingent on their becoming a citizen.

Noncitizenship apparently works for the military, so it may also be successful in law enforcement.

Having an awareness of diversity is certainly necessary as far as law enforcement leaders are concerned when it involves balanced hiring, staffing, and other personnel issues. The realization is even more important when it concerns the agency's involvement with the public.

Depending on what part of the nation your jurisdiction is located in, you can be sure that your citizenry will be made up of a diverse group with regard to race, religion, gender, ethnicity, and sexual preference, among others. This doesn't include the social, cultural, and political diversity that will also be present.

SOMEONE ONCE SAID:

Ethnic minorities are not one homogeneous political group.
—Rishi Sunak

As Ms. Diop said, achieving diversity is certainly going to be interesting.

In spite of the increased efforts at community relations, community policing programs, and similar struggles to improve the police image, racial and ethnic issues seem to be worsening. It is being alleged that ill-treatment of minorities by the police is systemic and cannot be allowed to continue.

These allegations are coming from Hollywood celebrities, civic and political leaders, and others.

SOMEONE ONCE SAID:

**There's a lot of things that need to change.
One specifically? Police brutality.**
—Colin Kaepernick

This increasing antipolice movement is currently centered on police/minority shootings. Even when investigation discloses the shooting was justified, protests that escalate into riots and insurrection accompanied by looting often occur. All the more reason to make sure that your agency's policies and capabilities regarding civil disturbances are current.

Here again, social media plays a large part in creating this climate of mistrust and unrest. Millions of people are informed and often misinformed of actions taken by law enforcement, and most often the message is a negative one and the factual nature of the information is seldom questioned.

Unlike professional media, social media has no obligation to attempt accuracy and no recourse is available for inaccuracy.

Even so, you must accept that it is the right of citizens to lawfully demonstrate against government actions perceived to be wrong. And it is law enforcement's responsibility to permit and control peaceful protest.

SOMEONE ONCE SAID:

One has a moral responsibility to disobey unjust laws.

—*Martin Luther King Jr.*

FINALLY

As the leader of a law enforcement agency you have a tremendous responsibility. First to the public. Your actions and decisions will have a tremendous impact on the safety and quality of life of the community you serve. Your actions, more than anyone else's, will also determine the success of your agency.

Additionally, the example you set and the leadership you provide your subordinates will have a tremendous bearing on their careers and future.

You must set a positive example, provide professional and caring leadership, insist on your subordinates' complete honesty, and demand that they do the right thing by enforcing the laws firmly and fairly. If done, you will be a successful leader.

SOMEONE ONCE SAID:

The key to successful leadership is figuring out what needs to be done and providing appropriate guidance to those who do it.
—Author

IN CONCLUSION

Just some personal thoughts.

- In this book we have examined the thoughts, philosophies, and what was "said" by some of the legendary trailblazers in supervision, management, and executive leadership. If you can emulate and apply even some of their teachings, you will be better for it.

- Only a couple of the experts had any law enforcement experience, so added to their sound advice were several "Once upon a times" that reflected actual occurrences in actual law enforcement agencies. Hopefully, something can be learned from those experiences as well.

- You may have noticed that substantial attention was paid to the subject of change. It is my belief that the greatest problem that you will be facing in the future is *change*. No matter your current rank or position, change will impact your personal and professional life profoundly.

- You will witness more change in the next year than your parents did in their lifetime. How you deal with it will determine your success and happiness. Try to anticipate it, and unless it is disastrous, don't fight it, and even if distasteful, try to accept it and make the best of it.

- And not all change is negative. Technological advancements are occurring that will assist you in crime fighting.
- Some of you may remember when in the last century, the law enforcement world was devastated by the Escobedo and Miranda case decisions on preserving a suspect's rights to counsel and the mandatory advisement of those rights. Many thought that the ability to obtain a conviction had been eliminated. "You can't tell suspects that they have the right to remain silent and then expect them to confess." Yet by following the military meme "Improvise, adapt, and overcome," law enforcement was soon able to recover and conviction rates were unaffected.

SOMEONE ONCE SAID:

You have power over your mind, not outside events. Realize this and you will find strength.
—Marcus Aurelius

- You must maintain a positive attitude. Every day may not be a pleasant one, but as bad as things may seem, you have the knowledge and experience to win.
- In our current social climate it will seem that you are unappreciated by the public, and oftentimes it will appear that people are taking sides with the bad guys. Don't lose heart; remember that you are providing an important service, and even though they don't always demonstrate it, the people depend on you. Be safe!

SOMEONE ONCE SAID:

We will be known by the tracks we leave.
—Lakota Indian proverb

CITED REFERENCES

Clayton Alderfer, *Existence, Relatedness, and Growth: Human Needs in Organizational Settings* (New York: Free Press, 1972).

James Belasco, *Teaching the Elephant to Dance* (New York: Crown, 1990).

Warren Bennis and Burt Nanus, *Leaders: The Strategies for Taking Charge* (New York: Harper & Row, 1985).

_____ , *On Becoming a Leader* (New York: Basic Books, 1989).

Ken Blanchard and Spencer Johnson, *The One Minute Manager* (New York: William Morrow, 1982).

Lewis Carroll, *Alice's Adventures in Wonderland* (London: Macmillan, 1865).

Michael Connelly, *The Gods of Guilt* (Boston: Little, Brown, 2013).

Stephen R. Covey, *The 7 Habits of Highly Effective People* (New York: Free Press, 1989).

Charles Darwin, *On the Origin of Species* (London: John Murray, 1859).

Edward M. Davis, *Staff One: A Perspective on Police Management* (Englewood Cliffs, NJ: Prentice-Hall, 1978).

Keith Davis, *Human Behavior at Work: Human Relations and Organizational Behavior* (New York: McGraw-Hill, 1971).

Wayne L. Davis, *Police-Community Relations: Bridging the Gap* (Bloomington, IN: Xlbris, 2015).

Edward Deci and Richard Ryan, *Intrinsic Motivation and Self-Determination in Human Behavior* (New York: Plenum, 1985).

Alfred DeCrane Jr., "A Constitutional Model of Leadership," in *The Leader of the Future,* ed. Frances Hesselbein, Marshall Goldsmith, and Richard Beckhard (San Francisco: Jossey-Bass, 1996).

Edwin Delattre, *Character and Cops* (Washington, DC: American Enterprise Institute, 2011).

W. Edwards Deming, *Out of the Crisis* (Cambridge, MA: Massachusetts Institute of Technology, Center for Advanced Educational Service, 1982).

Peter Drucker, *The Effective Executive* (New York: Harper & Row, 1967).

Kevin Eikenberry, *Leadership & Learning,* https://blog.kevineikenberry.com.

Harrington Emerson, *The Twelve Principles of Efficiency* (New York: The Engineering Magazine, 1912).

Henri Fayol, *General and Industrial Management,* trans. C. Storrs (London: Sir Isaac Pitman & Sons, 1949).

G. Patrick Gallagher, *Risk Management Behind the Blue Curtain* (Alexandria, VA: Public Risk Management Association, 1992).

Saul W. Gellerman, *Motivation in the Real World* (New York: Dutton, 1992).

William Glasser, *Reality Therapy in Action* (New York: Harper & Row, 1965).

Marshall Goldsmith, *What Got You Here Won't Get You There* (New York: Hyperion, 2007).

Luther Gulick, "Notes on the Theory of Organization," in *Papers on the Science of Administration,* ed. Luther Gulick and Lyndall Urwick (New York: Institution of Public Administration, 1937).

Frederick Herzberg, *Motivation to Work* (Abingdon-on-Thames, UK: Routledge, 1993).

John Huberman, "Discipline Without Punishment," *Harvard Business Review* (July-August 1964): 62.

Thomas Owen Jacobs, *Leadership and Exchange in Formal Organizations,* vol. 10 (Alexandria, VA: Human Resources Research Organization [humRRO], 1971).

Spencer Johnson, *Who Moved My Cheese?* (New York: G. P. Putnam's Sons, 1998).

Al Kaltman, *Cigars, Whiskey and Winning: Leadership Lessons from Ulysses S. Grant* (Paramus, NJ: Prentice-Hall, 1998).

W. Rolfe Kerr, "The Words of Christ—Our Spiritual Liahona," *174th Annual General Conference of the Church of Jesus Christ of Latter-day Saints* (Salt Lake City: Church of Jesus Christ of the Latter-day Saints, 2004).

James Kouzes and Barry Posner, *Credibility: How Leaders Gain and Lose It, Why People Demand It* (San Francisco: Jossey-Bass, 2011).

Michael LeBoeuf, *GMP: The Greatest Management Principle in the World* (New York: Berkley Publishing Group, 1989).

Otto Lerbinger, *Corporate Public Affairs* (Mahwah, NJ: Lawrence Erlbaum Associates, 2006).

Dean Ludwig and Clinton Longenecker, "The Bathsheba Syndrome:

The Ethical Failure of Successful Leaders," *Journal of Business Ethics* 12 (1993): 265–73.

Maxwell Maltz, *Psycho-Cybernetics* (New York: Prentice-Hall, 1960).

Abraham Maslow, "A Theory of Human Motivation," *Psychological Review* 50, no. 4 (1943): 265–73.

Elton Mayo, *The Human Problems of an Industrial Civilization* (New York: Macmillan, 1933).

John C. Maxwell, *Winning with People* (Nashville, TN: 2004).

_____ , *The 360 Degree Leader* (Nashville, TN: 2005).

David McClelland, *The Achieving Society* (New York: D. van Nostrand, 1961).

Douglas McGregor, *The Human Side of Enterprise* (New York: McGraw-Hill, 1960).

Robert Needham, *Team Secrets of the Navy SEALs* (New York: Skyhorse, 2003).

William H. Newman, *Administrative Action* (Hoboken, NJ: Second edition/ marginalia,1963).

George S. Odiorne, *Management by Objectives: A System of* Managerial Leadership (London: Pitman, 1965).

Taiichi Ohno, *Workplace Management* (New York: McGraw-Hill, 2013).

C. Northcote Parkinson, *Parkinson's Law: The Pursuit of Progress* (London: John Murray, 1958).

Ivan Pavlov, *Conditioned Reflexes* (London: Oxford University Press, 1927).

Norman Vincent Peale, *The Power of Positive Thinking* (New York: Simon & Schuster, 1952).

Laurence J. Peter, The Peter Principle (New York: William Morrow, 1969).

_____ , *The Peter Prescription* (New York: Bantam, 1972).

Tom Peters and Robert H. Waterman *In Search of Excellence* (New York: Harper & Row, 1982).

_____ , *Thriving on Chaos* (New York: Alfred A. Knopf, 1987).

Elaine D. Pulakos, *Performance Management* (Malden, MA: Wiley-Blackwell, 2009).

Everett Rogers, *Diffusion of Innovations* (New York: Free Press, 1962).

Herbert Simon, *Models of Discovery* (Dordrecht, The Netherlands: Reidel, 1977).

B. F. Skinner, *Science and Human Behavior* (New York: Macmillan, 1953).

Frederick Winslow Taylor, *The Principles of Modern Management* (New York: Harper & Brothers, 1911).

Noel M. Tichy and Mary Anne Devanna, *The Transformational Leader* (New York: John Wiley & Sons, 1986).

Sun Tzu and Samuel B. Griffith, *The Art of War* (Oxford: Clarendon Press, 1964).

Denis Waitley, *The Winner's Edge* (New York: New York Times Books, 1980).

Max Weber, *The Theory of Social and Economic Organization* (London: William Hodge, 1947).

Paul Whisenand and Jennifer McCain, *Managing Police Organizations*, 7th ed. (Upper Saddle River, NJ: Pearson Education, 2009).

Paul Whisenand, *Supervising Police Personnel: Strengths-Based Leadership*, 8th ed (Upper Saddle River, NJ: Pearson Education, 2014) .

O. W. Wilson, *Police Administration* (New York: McGraw-Hill, 1963).

Lorin Woolfe, *Leadership Secrets from the Bible* (New York: MJF Books, 2002).

Leonard Zunin and Natalie Zunin, *Contact: The First Four Minutes* (New York: Ballantine, 1982).

INDEX

ABOUT THE AUTHOR

John Anderson's first supervisory position was as a sergeant in the U.S. Army at age 19. Following his discharge from the military, Anderson began a 52-year career in law enforcement, rising from a police officer in his small home town to a Chief in the California Highway Patrol. During his 35-year career in the CHP, Anderson served as Commander of the CHP Central Division, consisting of 17 field commands in nine counties. As a Captain, he was the Commander of the CHP Academy. Anderson also served as a legislative liaison in Sacramento and Washington, D.C.

After retiring from the CHP, Anderson was elected and served four terms as Sheriff of Madera County. Following that he functioned as a District Representative for California State Senator Anthony Cannella. Anderson has also worked as a management consultant for the International Association of Chiefs of Police and conducted studies of several state law enforcement agencies. He holds a master's degree in public administration and has taught police management at the university level.

Anderson is the author of *The Newhall Incident*, a true crime account of the worst shooting in CHP history, which left four CHP officers dead.

He and his wife Kathy, a retired teacher, live on the Central Coast of California.

CPSIA information can be obtained
at www.ICGtesting.com
Printed in the USA
JSHW041950160522
25979JS00001B/22